Follow Up Activities

CONTENTS

Reading and writing numbers to 100 000   2

Relating operations   3

Using doubling and halving   4

Extending written methods for multiplication   5

Working with mixed numbers   6

Using decimal notation   7

Discussing chance or likelihood   8

Working with a bar chart   9

Reading co-ordinates   10

Calculating perimeter   11

Measuring to the nearest millimetre   12

Reading 24-hour times   13

Solving word problems: measurement   14

Finding a difference by counting up   15

Solving word problems: money   16

Identifying factors   17

Recognising patterns   18

Using symbols <, =, >, ≤, ≥   19

Multiplying by a number close to 20   20

Extending written methods for division   21

Solving real-life problems: money   22

Checking calculations   23

Ordering fractions   24

Ordering decimals   25

Identifying and measuring acute and obtuse angles   26

Calculating angles in a straight line   27

Investigating patterns made by rotating shapes   28

Using square centimetres   29

Relating grams to the kilogram   30

Interpreting data in a line graph   31

Extending written methods for decimals   32

Applying tests for divisibility   33

Developing calculator skills   34

Expressing a quotient as a fraction or decimal   35

Using long multiplication   36

Solving real-life problems: money   37

Relating fractions and decimals   38

Finding a simple percentage of a whole number   39

Working with ratio and proportion   40

Finding the mode and range   41

Reflecting shapes in one or two lines   42

Making translations   43

Using a bus timetable   44

Knowing the relationships between units of capacity   45

Adding three or more numbers   46

Solving real-life problems: percentages   47

Finding pairs of factors   48

Name ....

Finish the puzzles.
(Show each number on the expander, in figures and in words.)

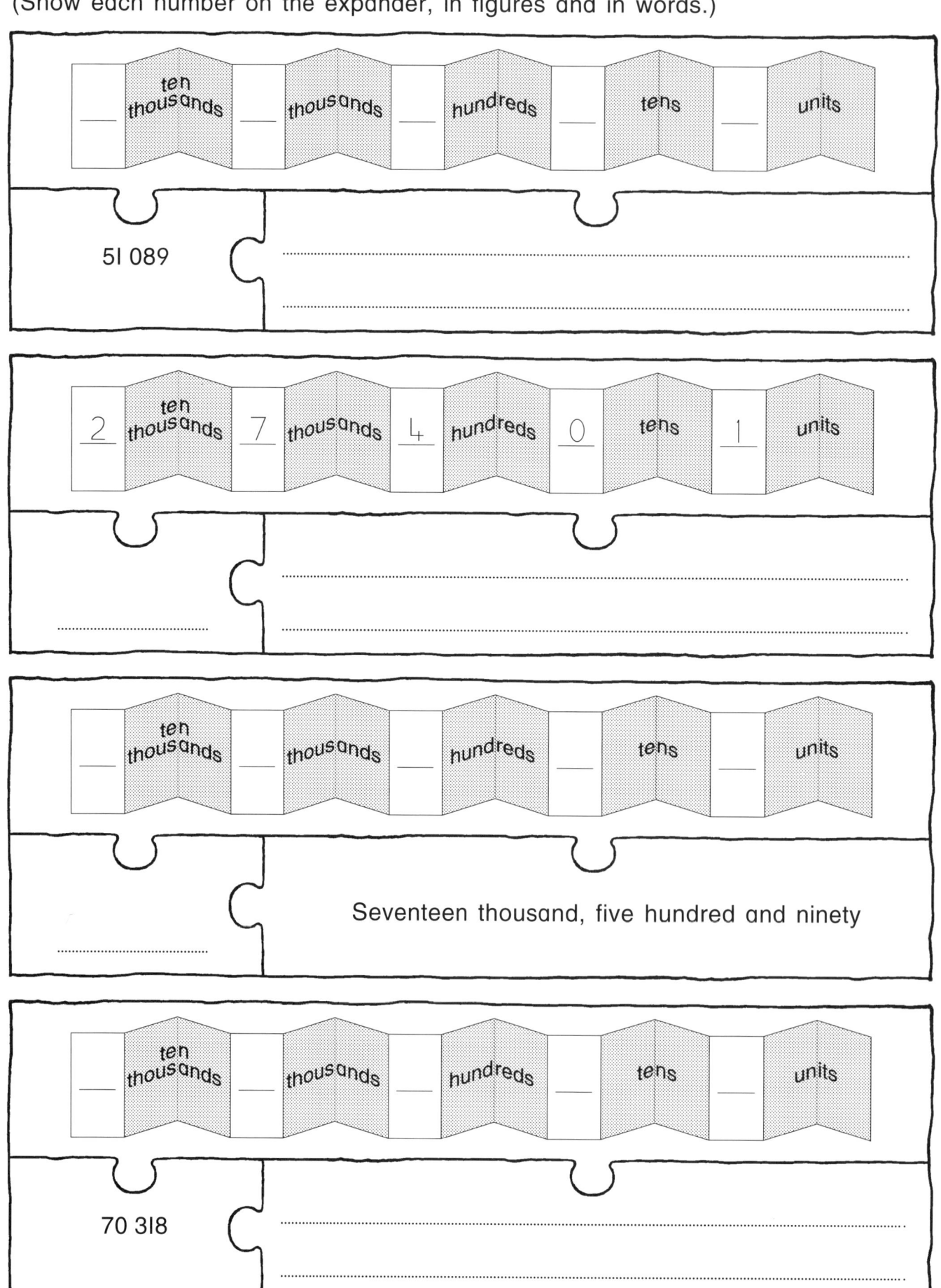

51 089

ten thousands	thousands	hundreds	tens	units
2	7	4	0	1

Seventeen thousand, five hundred and ninety

70 318

2 **Reading and writing numbers to 100 000**
(Follows *Giant Discussion Book* page 2.)

Name ....

Figure out the number of **layers** in each carton.
Show **two** different ways you could find each answer.

Name ....

Use the information in the table to solve the problems below.

Colour one of the ◯s to show whether you **doubled** or **halved**.

	MARGARINE	CHEESE	SALAMI
250 g	48p	86p	95p
500 g	92p	£1.70	£1.78
1 kg	£1.80	£2.35	£2.52

What is the cost of 2 [500g margarine]?

(Doubled) (Halved)

How much more than 1kg salami would 2 500g salami cost?

(Doubled) (Halved)

How much would you pay for 2 [1kg cheese]?

(Doubled) (Halved)

Which is the better buy, [1kg margarine] or 2 [500g margarine]?

(Doubled) (Halved)

Which is the better buy, 2 [250g cheese] or [500g cheese]?

(Doubled) (Halved)

Tim and Meg split the cost of [500g salami]. How much did each person pay?

(Doubled) (Halved)

Suppose you bought 2 [1kg cheese]. How much change from £5 would you get?

(Doubled) (Halved)

Is the price of [500g cheese] more or less than twice the price of [500g margarine]?

(Doubled) (Halved)

Do 4 [250g salami] cost more or less than [1kg salami]?

(Doubled) (Halved)

Using doubling and halving
(Follows *Giant Discussion Book* page 4.)

Name ....

Calculate the number of people these planes could carry each day.
Show your working.

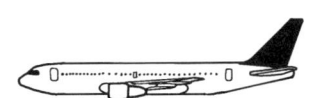

Seats 285.
4 flights each day.

Seats 348.
3 flights each day.

Seats 246.
5 flights each day.

Seats 336.
4 flights each day.

Seats 144.
6 flights each day.

Seats 428.
3 flights each day.

Extending written methods for multiplication
(Follows *Giant Discussion Book* page 5.)

Name ....

1. Count in steps to finish labelling the number lines.
(Write improper fractions **above** and mixed numbers **below** each line.)

Count in steps of **one half**

0 — 1/2 — 2/2 — 3/2 —
0 — 1/2 — 1 — 1½ —

Count in steps of **one quarter**

0 — 1/4 — 2/4 — — 4/4 — 5/4 —
0 — 1/4 — 2/4 — — 1 — 1¼ —

Count in steps of **one eighth**

0 — 1/8 — 2/8 — 3/8 — 4/8 — — — 8/8 — 9/8 —
0 — 1/8 — 2/8 — — — — — 1 — 1⅛ —

2. Write each of these numbers another way.

| 9/4 = | 13/8 = | 3¼ = | = 2⅝ | 7/2 = | = 3 |

Working with mixed numbers
(Follows *Giant Discussion Book* page 6.)

Name ....

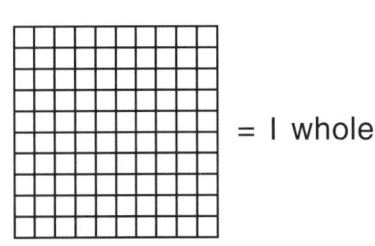 = 1 whole

1. Read the fraction name.
   Colour squares to match.
   Fill in the open and closed expanders.

two and thirty-five hundredths

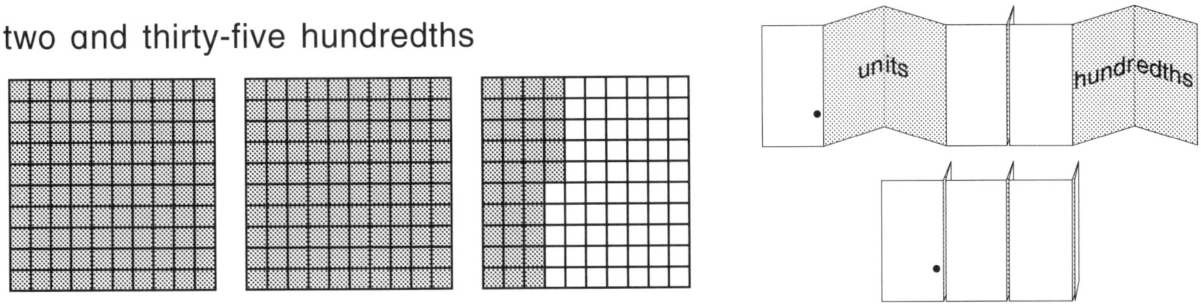

one and twenty-nine hundredths

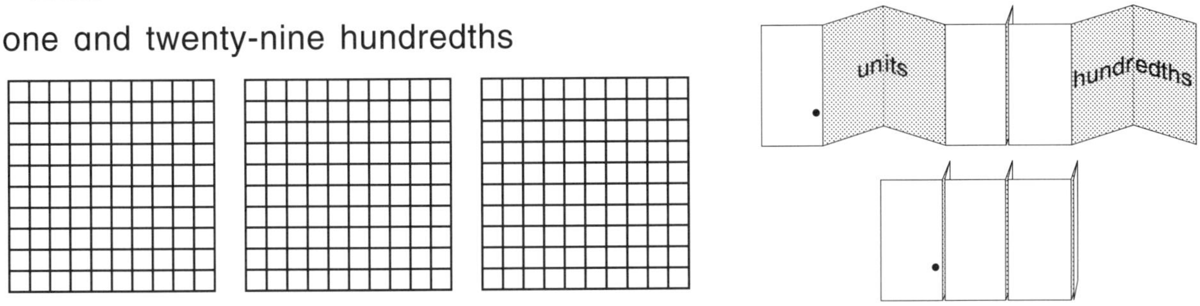

one and seventy-five hundredths

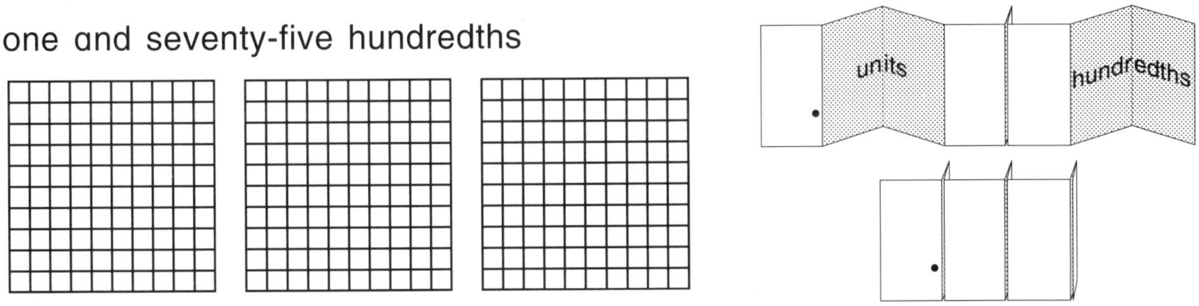

two and sixteen hundredths

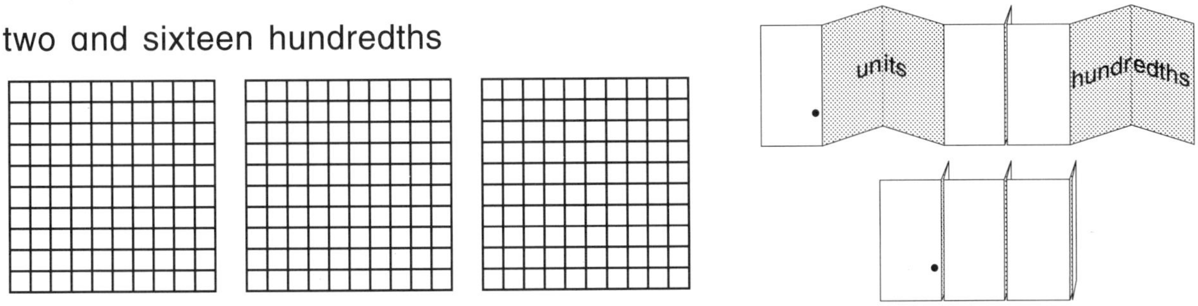

one and four hundredths

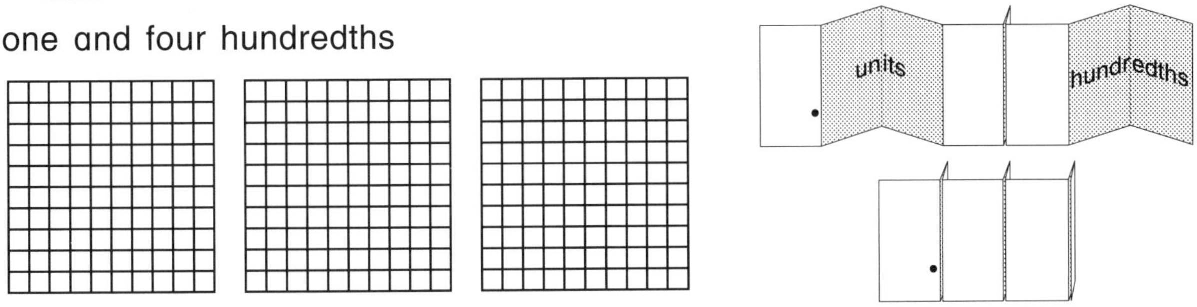

2. Loop the **tenths** digit in each decimal fraction.

Using decimal notation
(Follows *Giant Discussion Book* page 7.)

Name ....

Colour the spinners.

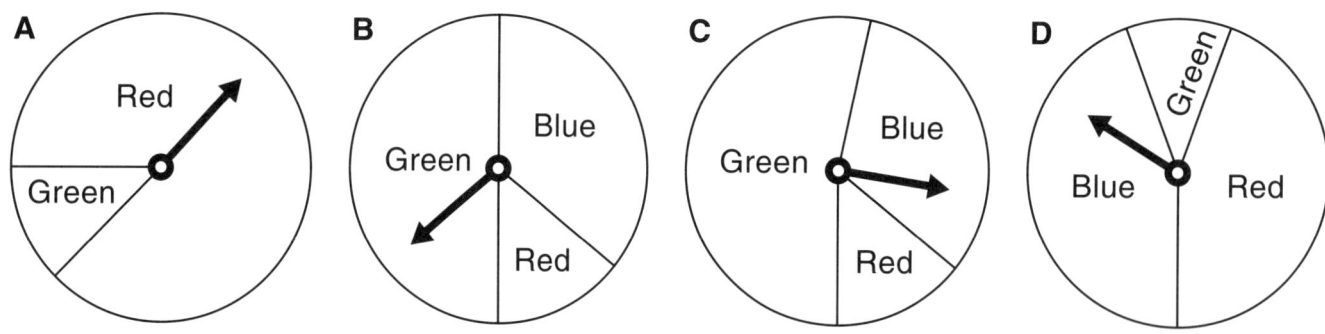

1. Draw and label an arrow to show each spinner's chance of stopping on these colours.

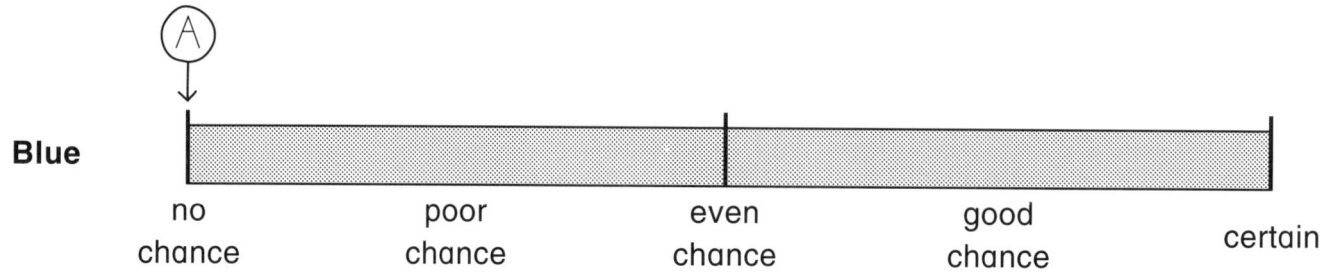

Blue

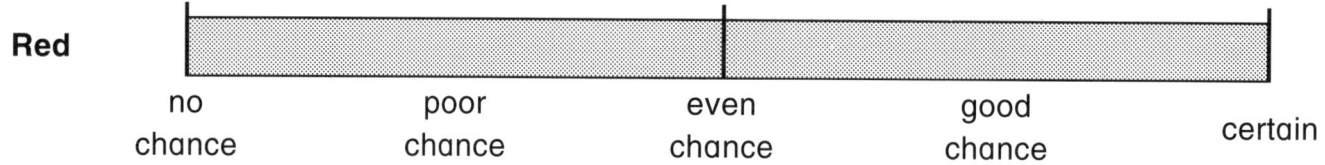

Red

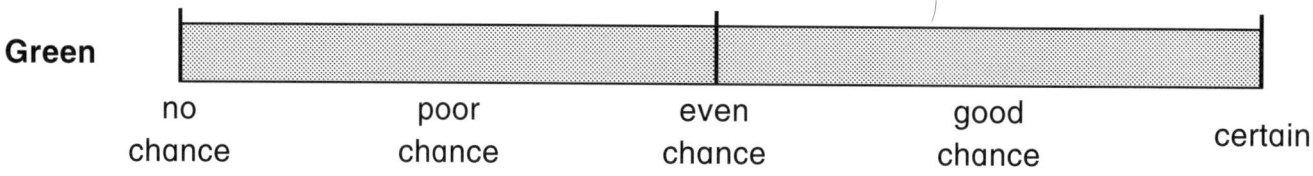

Green

2. Draw arrows to show the chance of these events happening tomorrow.

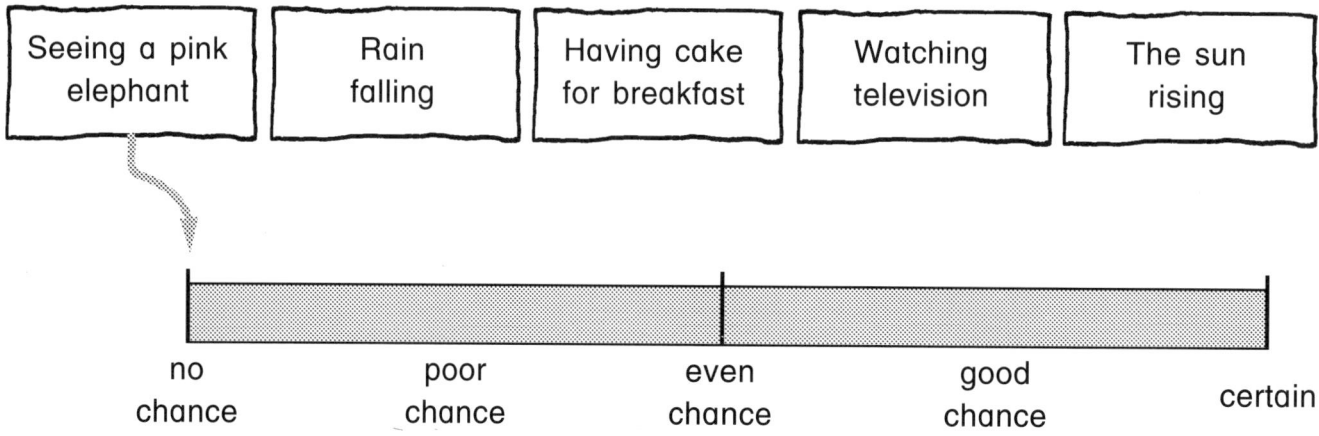

| 8 | **Discussing chance or likelihood**
(Follows *Giant Discussion Book* page 8.)

Name ....

1. Find the **total** attendance each day.
   Also figure out the **difference** between the number of children and adults.

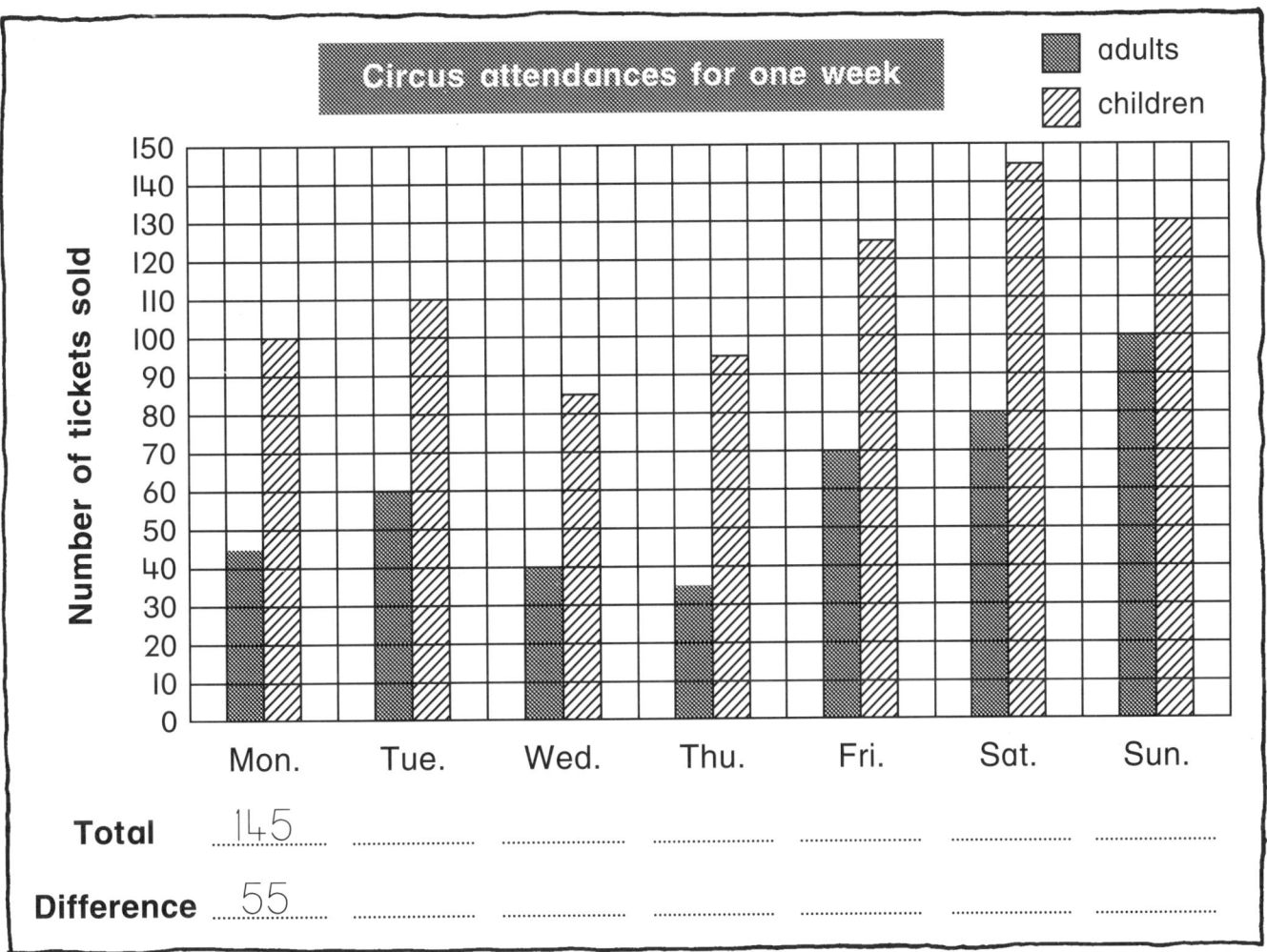

Total 145	....	....	....	....	....	....
Difference 55	....	....	....	....	....	....

2. Complete the story.

More children went to the circus on .... than any other day.

The most popular day for adults was .... The highest total

attendance was on .... and the lowest was on ....

On Sunday, sales of adults' tickets (£10 each) brought in .... pounds,

and children's tickets (£6 each) brought in .... pounds. That was

.... pounds altogether. During the whole week, more than ....

people went to the circus. The reason more children's tickets than adults'

tickets were sold each day was probably because ....

....

Working with a bar chart
(Follows *Giant Discussion Book* page 9.)

Name ....

1. For each shape, plot the points on the grid. Use a ruler to join them in order. Write the names of the shapes you know.

Shape	Points	Name
A	(5,4) → (12,4) → (10,8) → (3,8) → (5,4)	
B	(16,8) → (12,12) → (16,16) → (20,12) → (16,8)	
C	(3,15) → (2,12) → (3,9) → (10,12) → (3,15)	
D	(13,3) → (15,7) → (18,7) → (22,3) → (13,3)	
E	(4,17) → (4,19) → (21,19) → (21,17) → (4,17)	

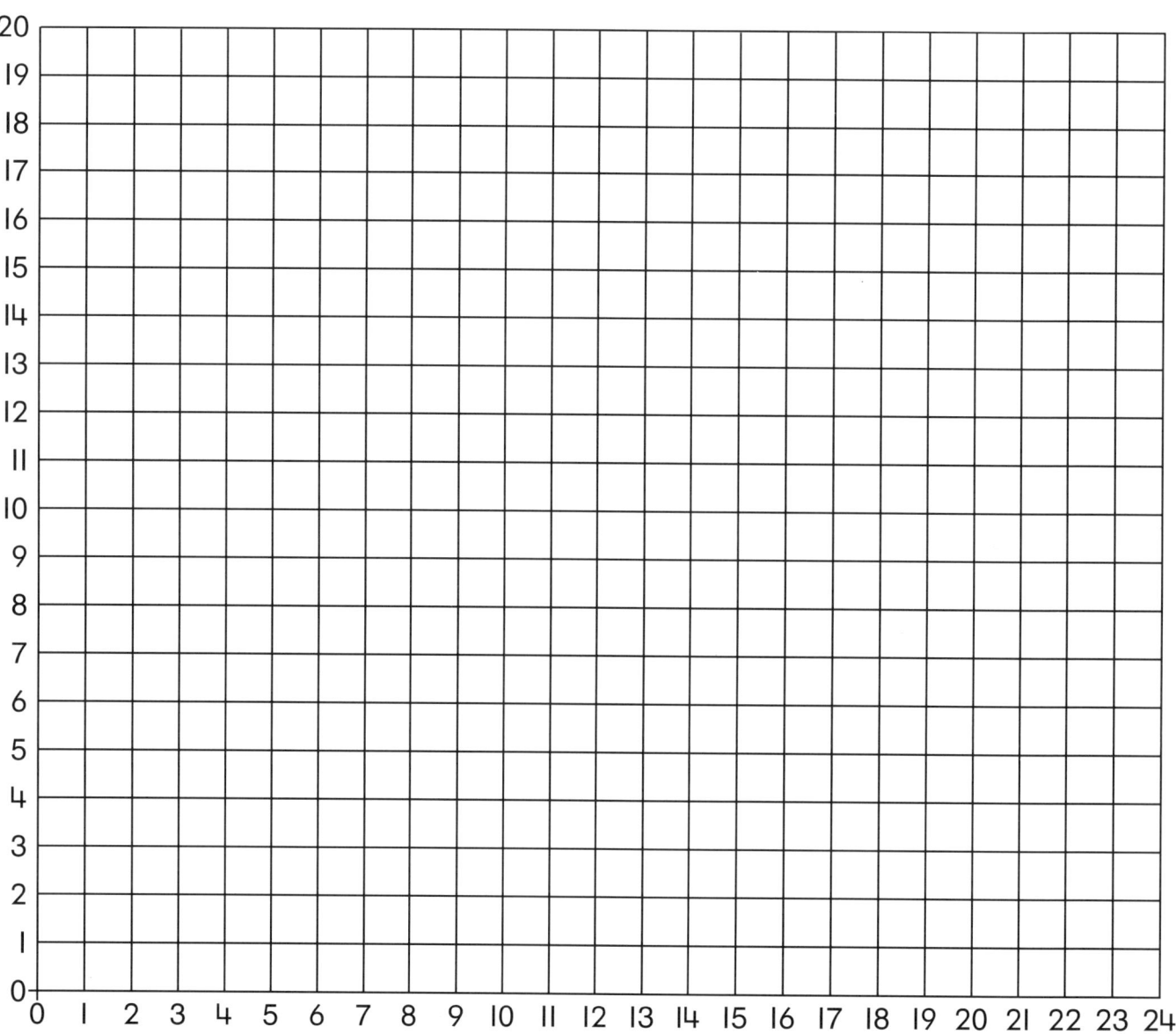

2. Mark pairs of **parallel** sides. (Use a colour that will show up well.)

Reading co-ordinates
(Follows *Giant Discussion Book* page 10.)

Name ....

1. Calculate the perimeters.

Perimeter of A = ... cm.   Perimeter of B = ... cm.

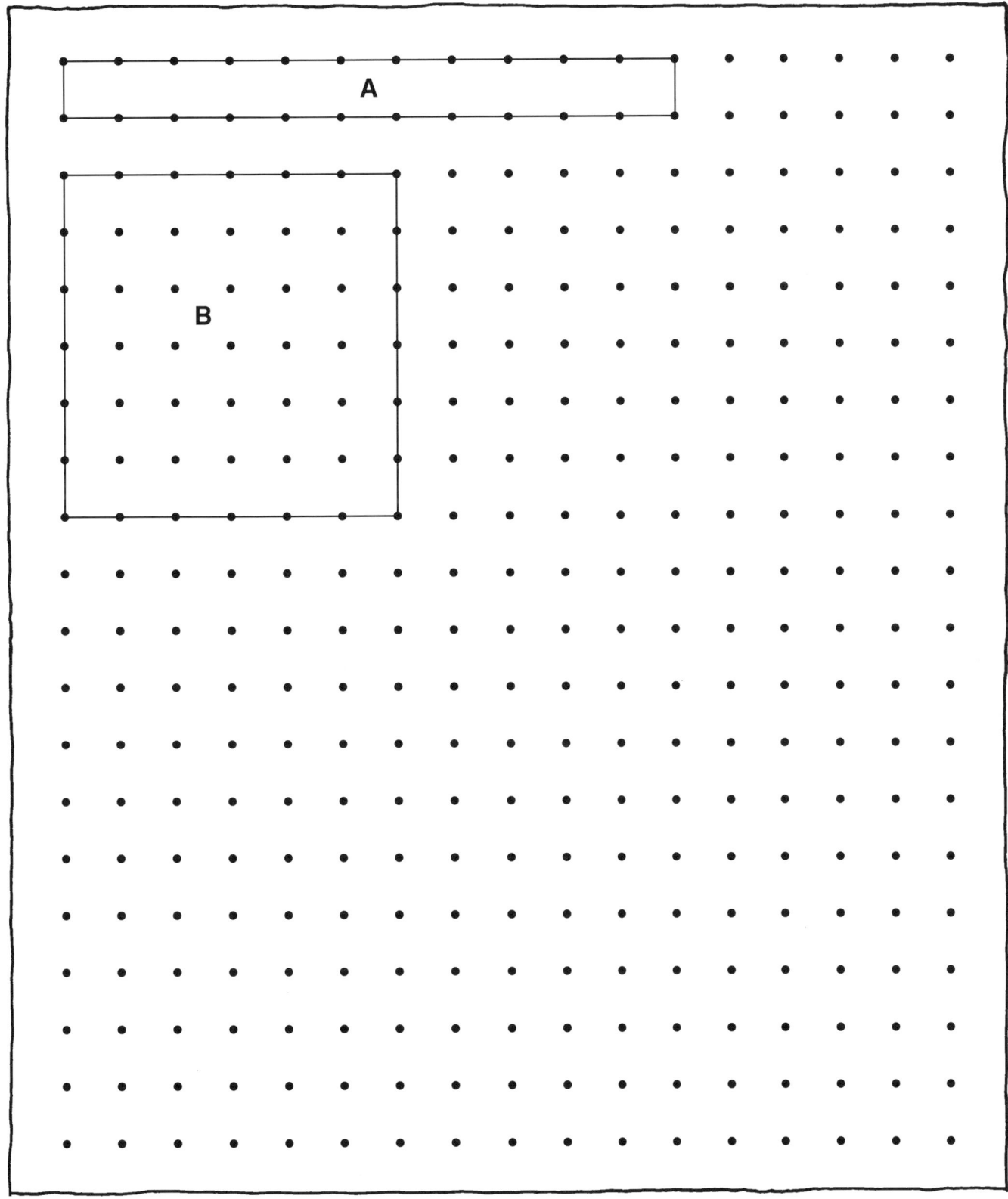

2. Draw four different rectangles that have the same perimeter as A and B.

3. On the back of this sheet, write the steps you would use to figure out the perimeter of a rectangle.

Calculating perimeter
(Follows *Giant Discussion Book* page 11.)

11

Name ....

Timber cross-sections		
Type	Width × Thickness	Picture
Decking	70 mm × 22 mm	
Flooring	120 mm × 19 mm	
Framing	75 mm × 45 mm	
Framing	75 mm × 35 mm	
Lining	140 mm × 12 mm	

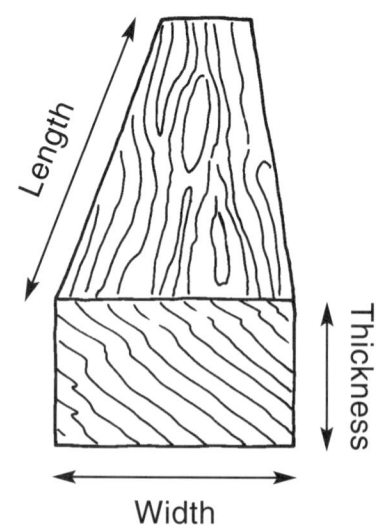

1. Estimate the width and thickness of each cross-section below.
   Match each of the pictures to a type of timber.
   (Write each letter in the table.)

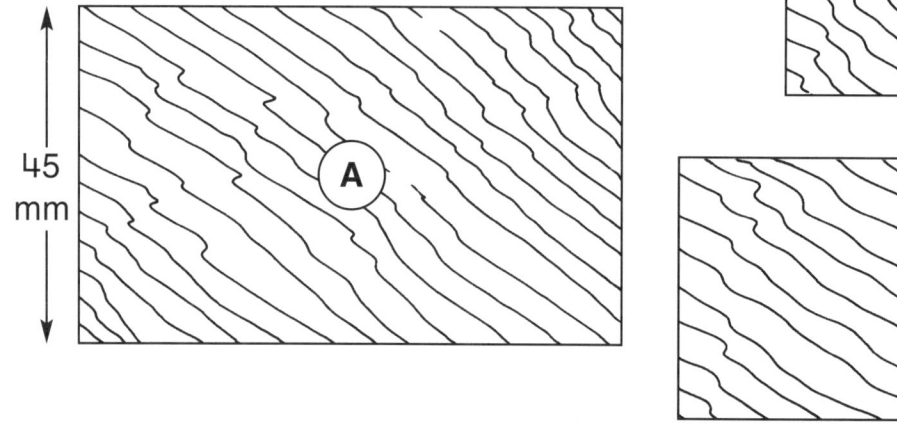

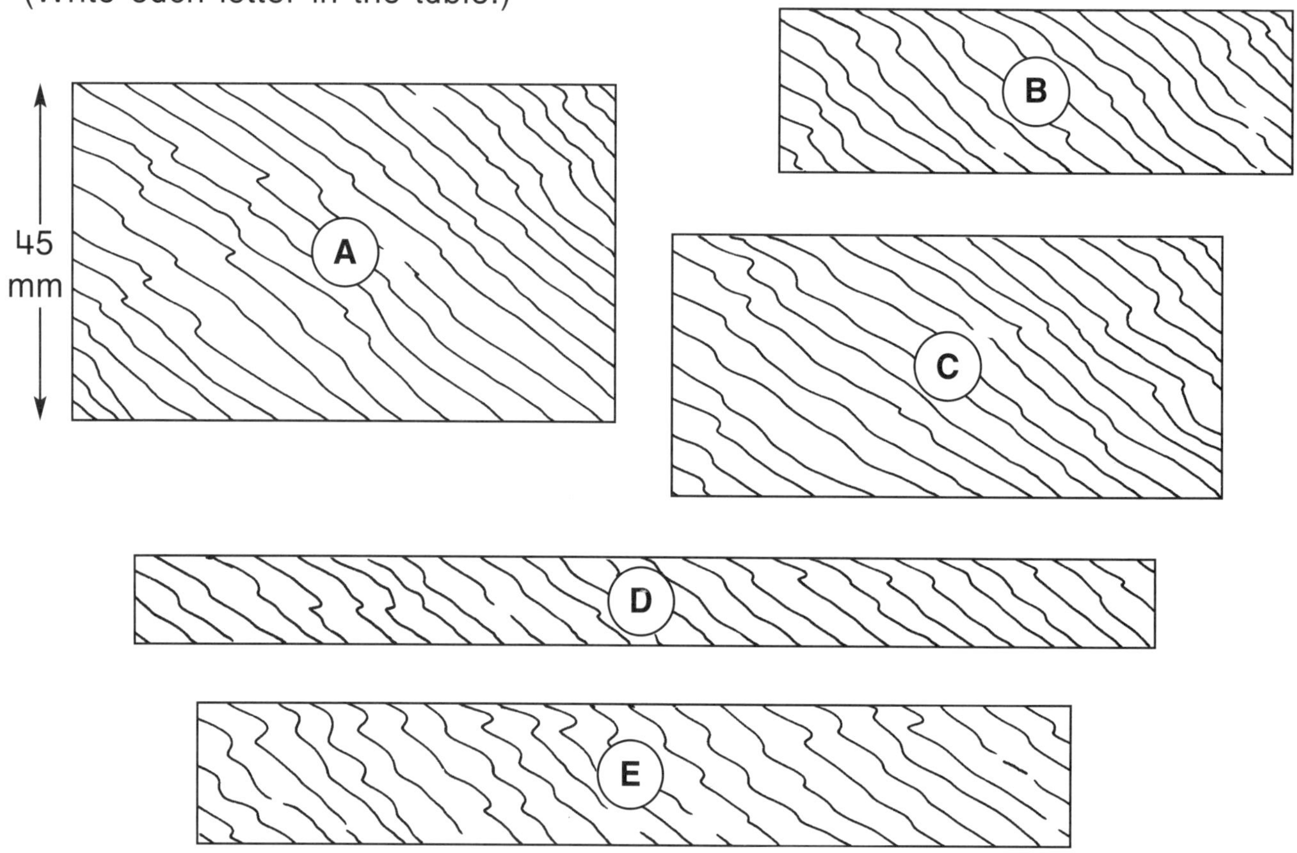

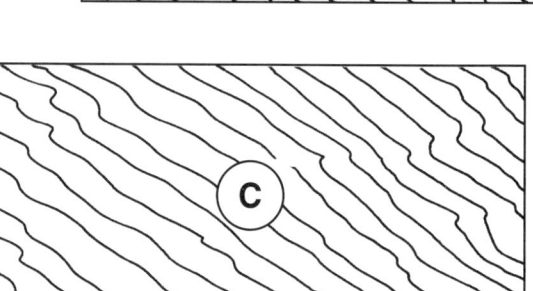

2. Measure each width and thickness to check your answers.

3. On the reverse side of this sheet, draw cross-sections that measure:

90 mm × 45 mm	45 mm × 45 mm	150 mm × 25 mm

12 **Measuring to the nearest millimetre**
(Follows *Giant Discussion Book* page 12.)

Name _____

1. Write the missing times.

12-hour clock	24-hour clock
12:00 midnight	00:00
1:00 a.m.	1:00
	10:00
12:00 noon	
	14:00
	23:00
12:00 midnight	00:00

2. Show each 24-hour time on the clock-face. Loop **a.m.** or **p.m.** Write what you might be doing at that time.

24-hour clock	12-hour clock
07:35 — At this time, I	a.m. p.m.
13:15 — At this time, I	a.m. p.m.
17:55 — At this time, I	a.m. p.m.
20:20 — At this time, I	a.m. p.m.

Reading 24-hour times

(Follows *Giant Discussion Book* page 13.)

Name ....

1. Complete the table.

Olympic swimming distances	Number of lengths of a 50-metre pool	Distance more or less than 1 km
50 metres	1	950 metres less
100 metres		
200 metres		
400 metres		
1500 metres		
4 × 100 metres (relay)	8	
4 × 200 metres (relay)		

2. Join each ◯ to **one** of the Olympic distances.

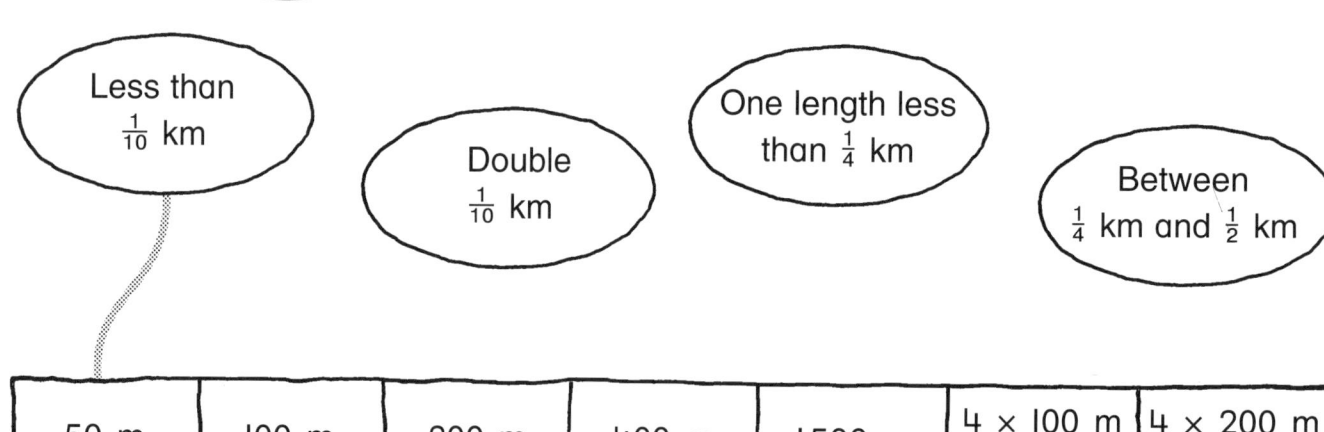

Solving word problems: measurement
(Follows *Giant Discussion Book* page 14.)

Name ....

British bridges

 Humber	 Firth of Forth (road)	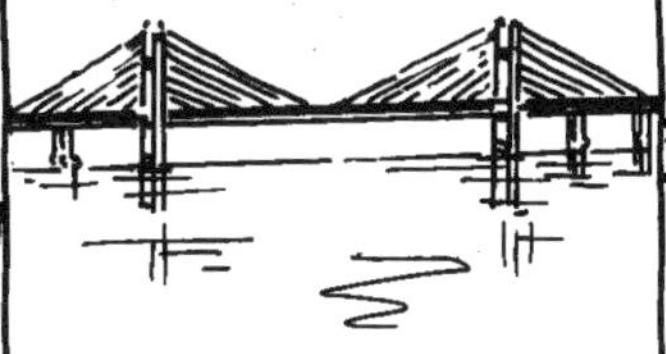 Severn	 Firth of Forth (rail)
1410 metres	1006 metres	988 metres	521 metres

Calculate the difference between the length of these bridges.
Show your working.

Firth of Forth (road) and Severn

.... metres

Humber and Firth of Forth (road)

.... metres

Humber and Severn

.... metres

Firth of Forth (road) and Firth of Forth (rail)

.... metres

Severn and Firth of Forth (rail)

.... metres

Finding a difference by counting up
(Follows *Giant Discussion Book* page 15.)

Name ....

Event	Film premiere	Outdoor theatre	Rock concert	Rugby match	Football match	Tennis final
Ticket price	£12.50	£36.00	£48.00	£15.75	£18.00	£31.25

Solve these problems. Show your working, and check your answers.

If you bought 2 rugby tickets, how much change would you get from £35?	How many tickets for the film premiere can you buy with £50?	Suppose you have £75. How much more do you need for 3 tickets to the tennis final?
How much would it cost for 6 football tickets?	The rock band receives half of the ticket sales. If you buy 6 tickets, how much goes to the band?	How much more would it cost 3 people to go to the rock concert rather than the outdoor theatre?

Solving word problems: money

(Follows *Giant Discussion Book* page 16.)

Name ....

To answer the riddle:
- colour the factors (to make letters)
- write the letters in order across the bottom of the sheet.

Riddle:
What do you get when you cross a dinosaur with a lemon?

Factors of 12
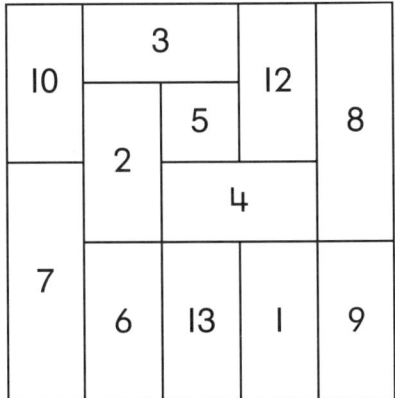

Factors of 18
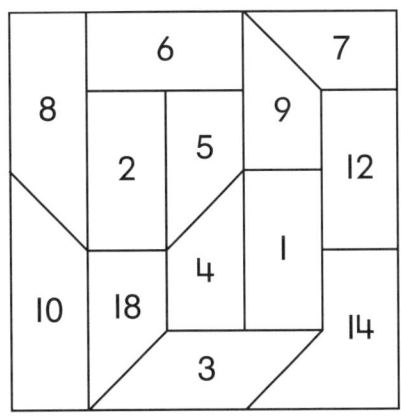

Factors of 25
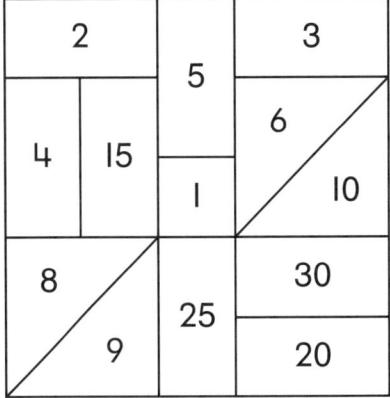

Factors of 30
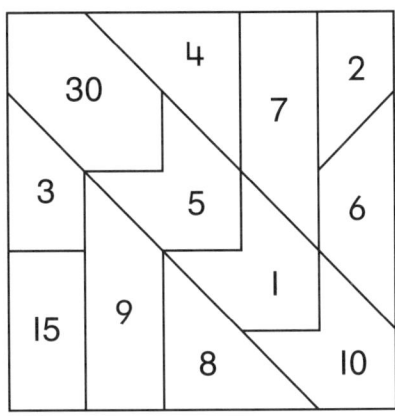

Factors of 33
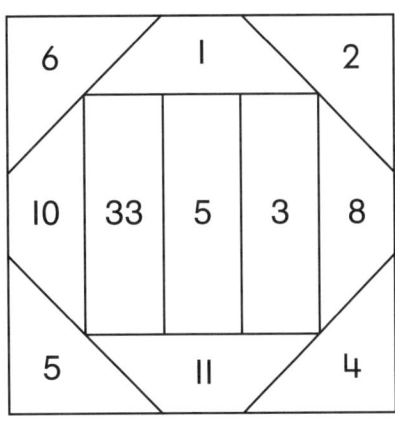

Factors of 16
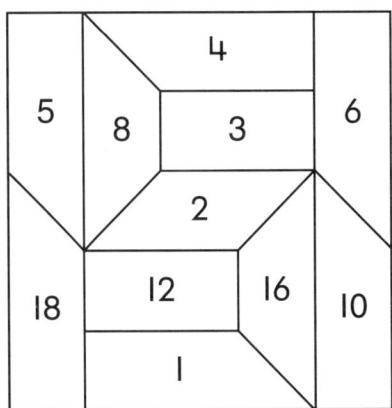

Factors of 42
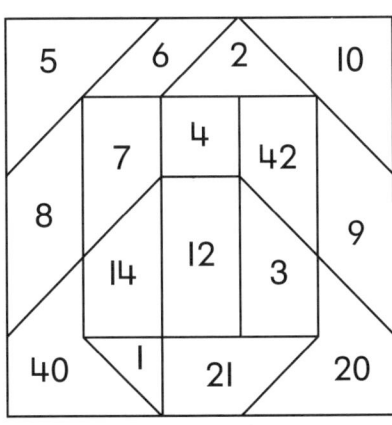

Factors of 45
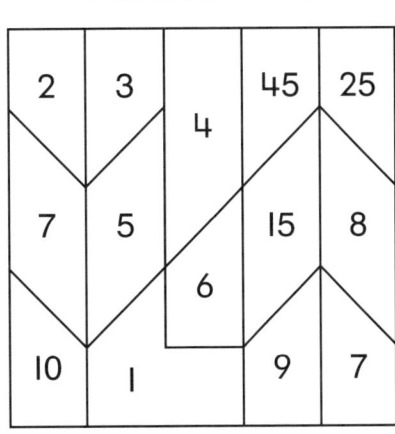

Factors of 64
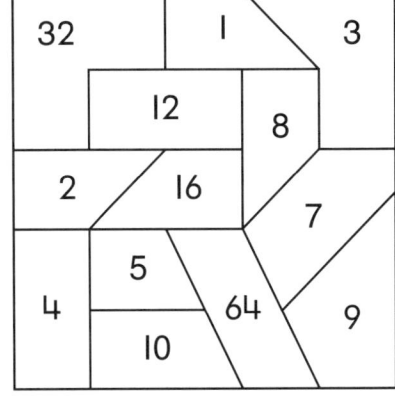

Answer: 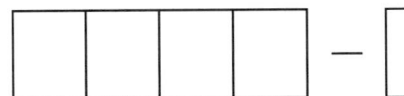 —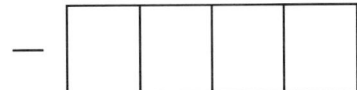

Identifying factors 17
(Follows *Giant Discussion Book* page 17.)

Name ....

1. Draw diagonals to divide each shape into triangles.
   (**Don't** let the diagonals cross each other.)
   Record the number of sides, diagonals and triangles in the table.

   A diagonal is a straight line that connects two corners of a shape. (It is not a side.)

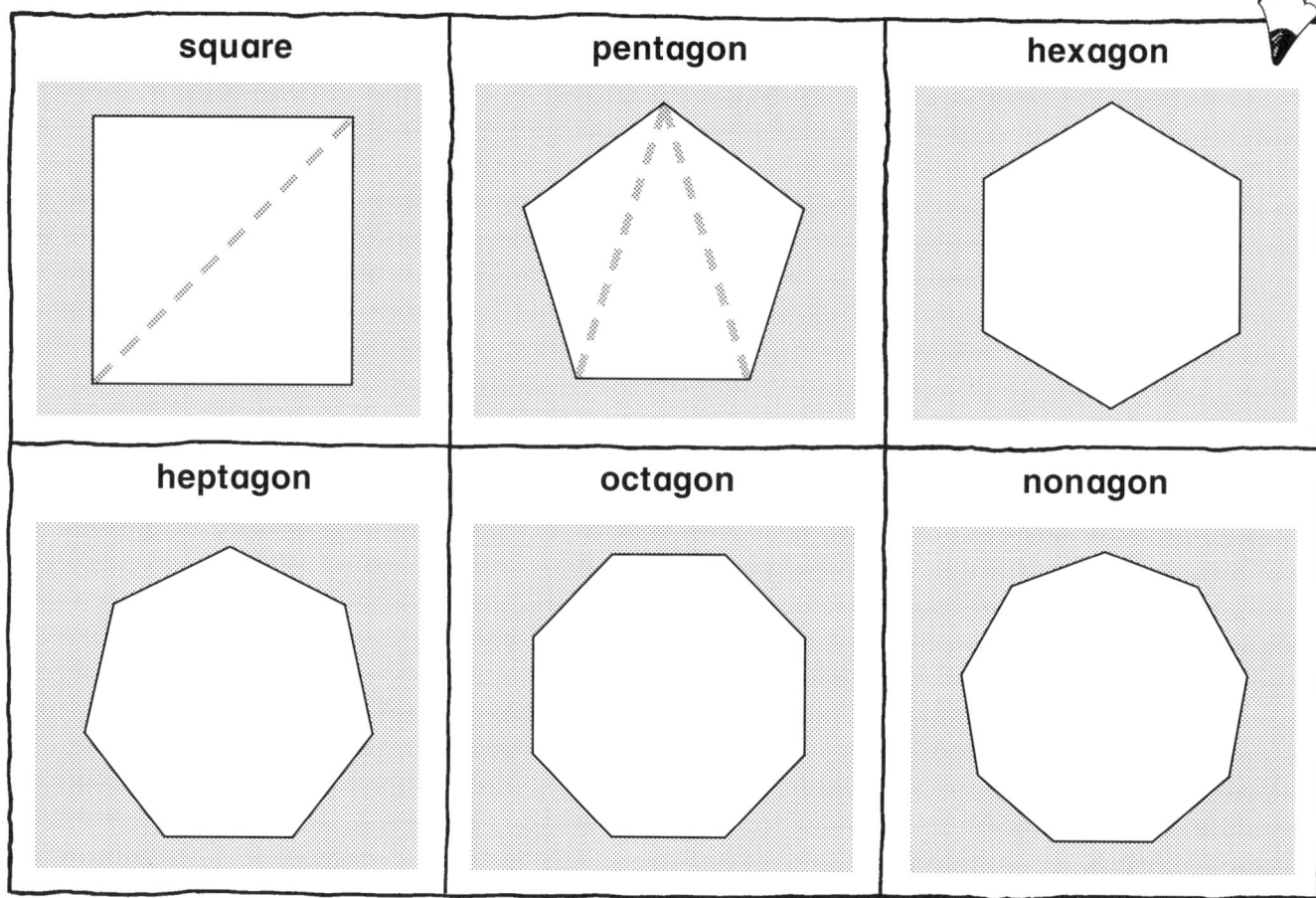

	square	pentagon	hexagon	heptagon	octagon	nonagon
Sides	4					
Diagonals	1					
Triangles	2					

2. Use the patterns in the table to predict the number of diagonals and triangles for:

a 10-sided shape	.... diagonals	.... triangles
a 100-sided shape	.... diagonals	.... triangles

Recognising patterns
(Follows *Giant Discussion Book* page 18.)

Name ....

1. Find each pair of countries in the table.
   Tick a box to show the country
   that published more books.
   Write the numbers in the correct order.

Books published in one year*	
Country	Number of titles
China	100 951
France	34 766
Germany	74 174
Italy	34 470
Korea, South	35 864
Netherlands	34 067
Russia	33 623
Spain	48 467
UK	101 764
USA	62 039

☐ Germany or ☐ Spain?

.... > ....

☐ Netherlands or ☐ Italy?

.... > ....

☐ China or ☐ UK?

.... > ....

*Based on figures for 1994 or 1995.
USA figure does not include text books.

2. Copy **both** numbers from the table.
   Write < or > in the box to make a true sentence.

France ☐ Spain	South Korea ☐ Netherlands
USA ☐ Germany	Russia ☐ Italy
UK ☐ China	France ☐ Italy

3. Write **true** or **false** for each of these.

32 715 > 32 751	46 205 < 46 250	34 766 ≤ 34 766	34 766 ≥ 34 766

Using symbols <, =, >, ≤, ≥
(Follows *Giant Discussion Book* page 19.)

Name ....

Fill the gaps to show the thinking used to multiply by **19** or **21**.

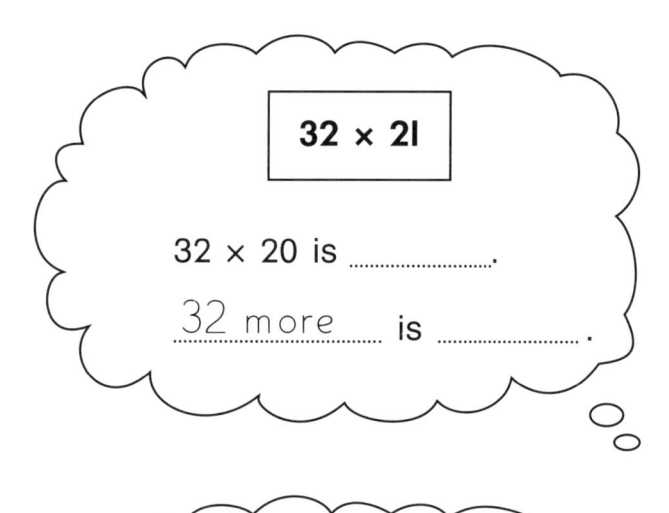

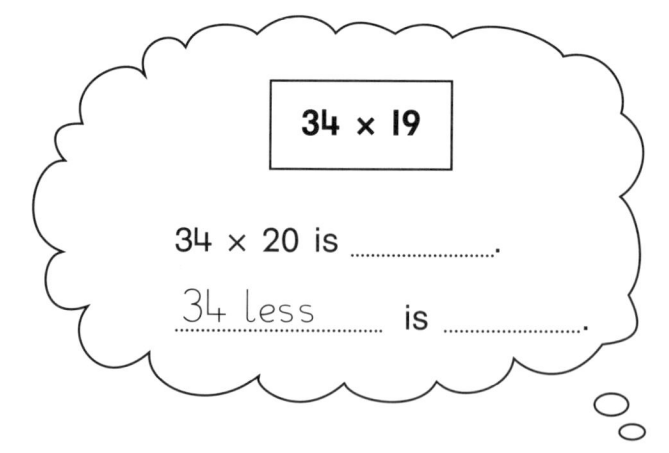

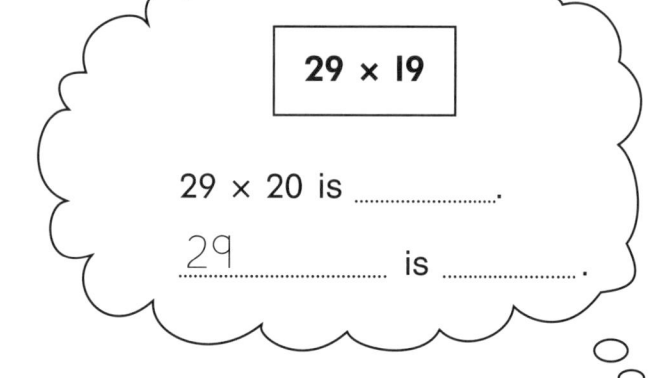

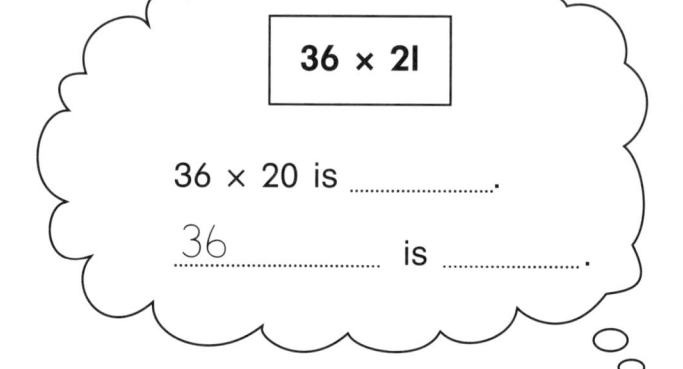

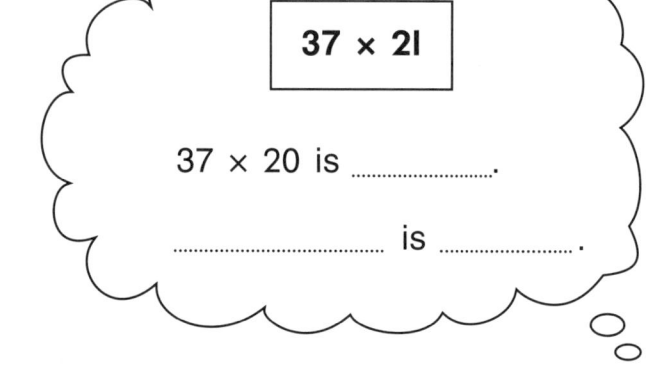

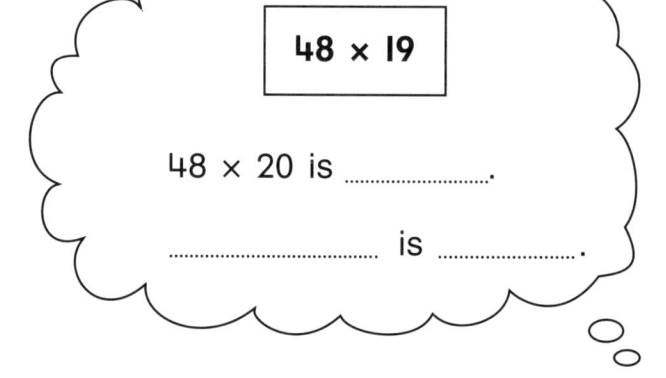

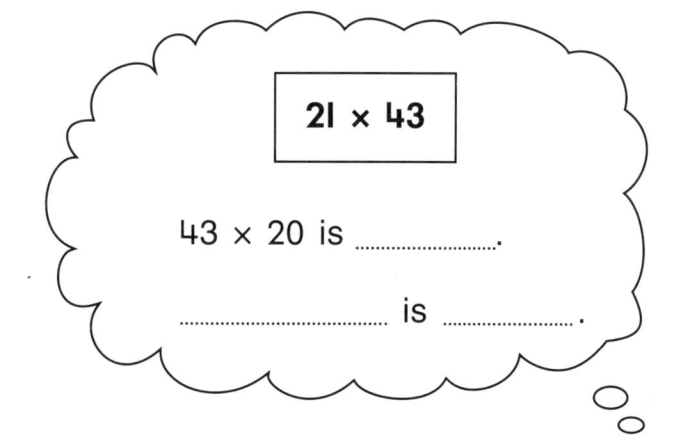

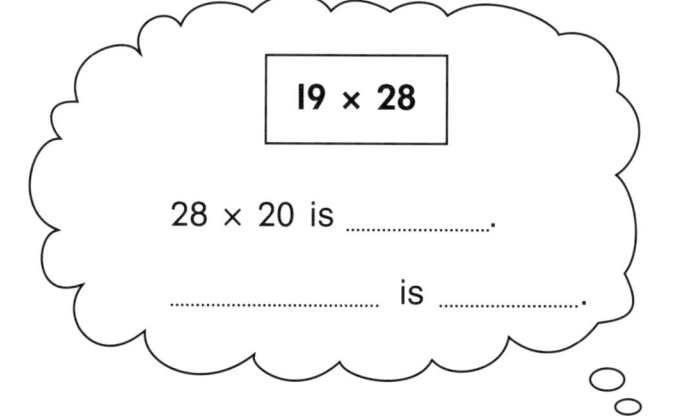

32 × 21

32 × 20 is ....
32 more is ....

34 × 19

34 × 20 is ....
34 less is ....

29 × 19

29 × 20 is ....
_29_ is ....

36 × 21

36 × 20 is ....
_36_ is ....

37 × 21

37 × 20 is ....
.... is ....

48 × 19

48 × 20 is ....
.... is ....

21 × 43

43 × 20 is ....
.... is ....

19 × 28

28 × 20 is ....
.... is ....

Multiplying by a number close to 20
(Follows *Giant Discussion Book* page 20.)

Name ....

Figure out the number of bags needed, and the number of sweets left over. Show your working.

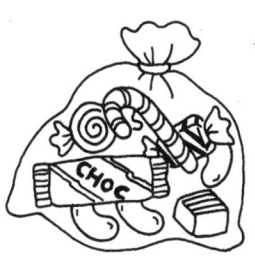

158 sweets	192 toffees	254 jelly beans
5 in each bag	4 in each bag	6 in each bag
Bags needed:	Bags needed:	Bags needed: ....
left over:	left over:	left over: ....
167 bars	254 caramels	375 candy canes
3 in each bag	5 in each bag	6 in each bag
Bags needed:	Bags needed:	Bags needed: ....
left over:	left over:	left over: ....

Extending written methods for division

(Follows *Giant Discussion Book* page 21.)

Name ....

1. Write the missing prices in the **first row** and **column** of the Ready Reckoner.

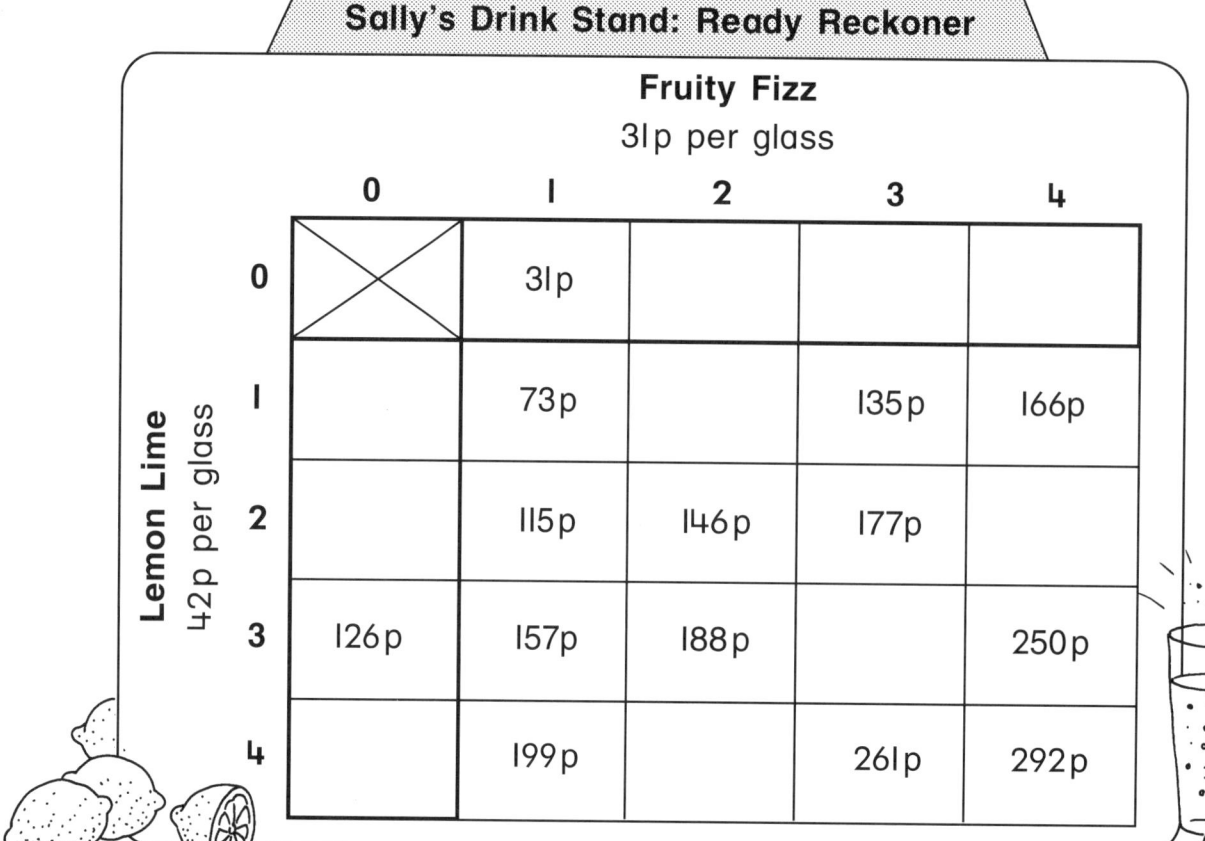

2. Use the Ready Reckoner to find the cost of these.

1 Fruity Fizz and 1 Lemon Lime	1 Fruity Fizz and 3 Lemon Lime	3 Fruity Fizz and 2 Lemon Lime	4 Fruity Fizz and 4 Lemon Lime
....	....	....	....

3. Figure out the missing prices in the Ready Reckoner. Show your working below. Write the answers in the chart.

2 Fruity Fizz and 1 Lemon Lime	4 Fruity Fizz and 2 Lemon Lime	3 Fruity Fizz and 3 Lemon Lime	2 Fruity Fizz and 4 Lemon Lime

Solving real-life problems: money
(Follows *Giant Discussion Book* page 22.)

Name ....

1. Colour the shapes where the answer is an **even** number.

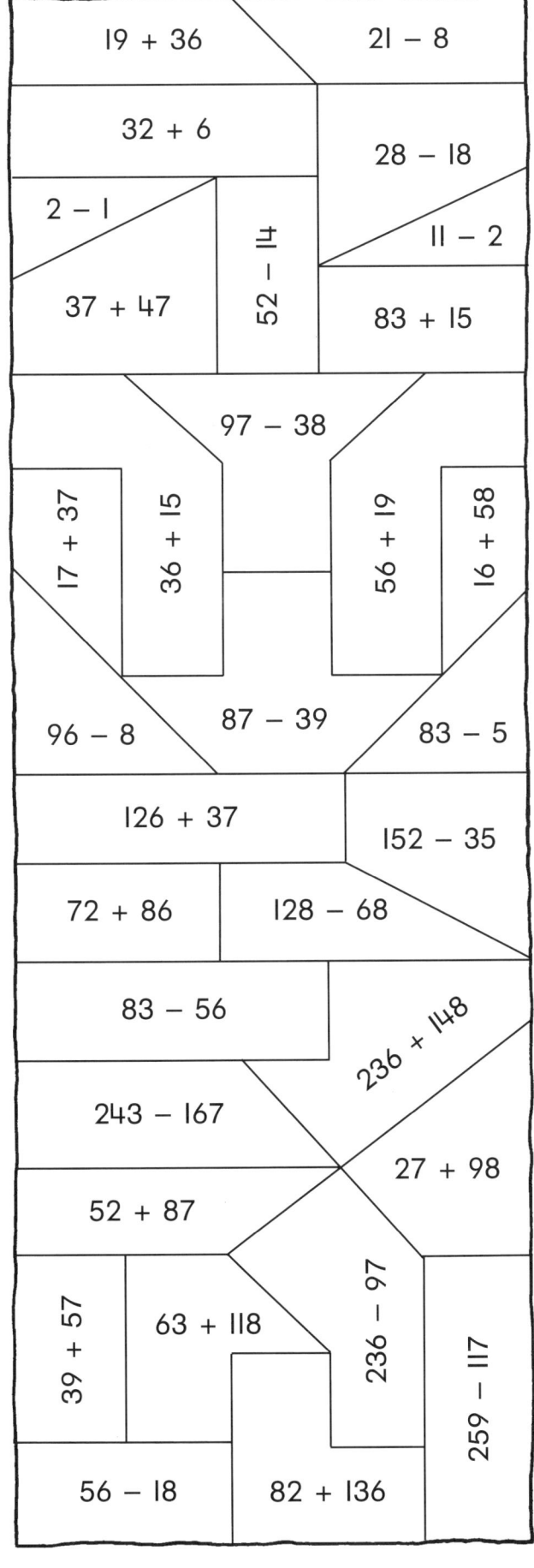

2. Colour the shapes where the answer is an **odd** number.

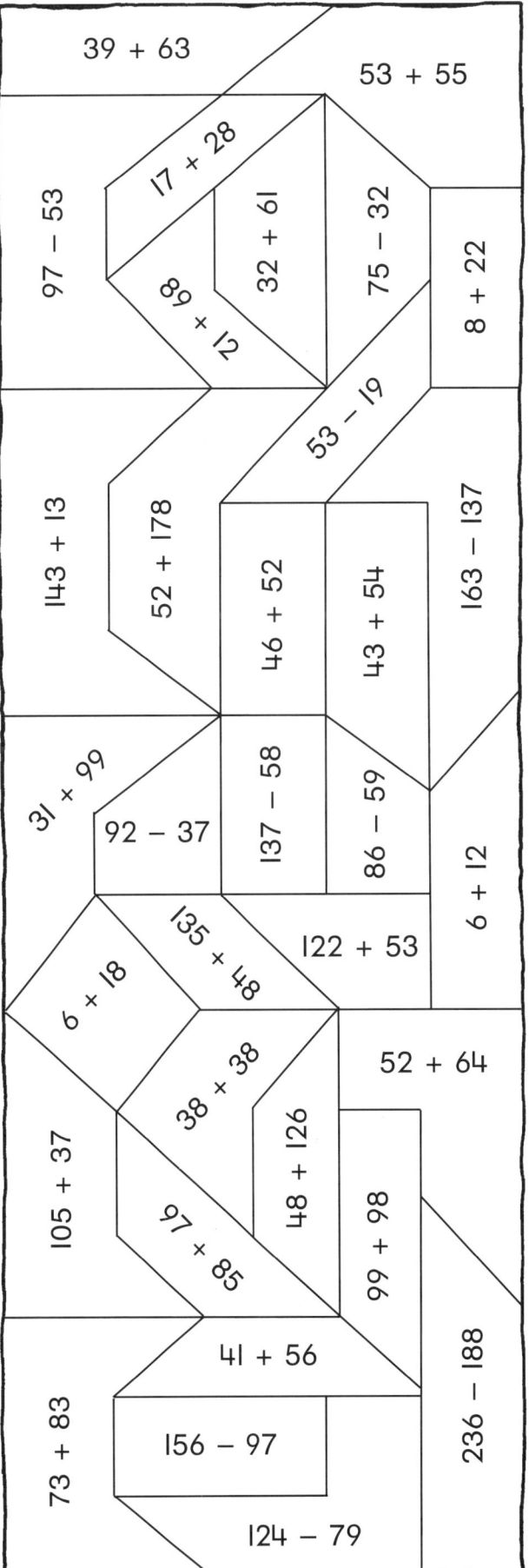

Checking calculations
(Follows *Giant Discussion Book* page 23.)

23

Name ....

1. Colour the first 'brick' in each row of the fraction wall.

1
½ ½
⅓ ⅓ ⅓
¼ ¼ ¼ ¼
⅕ ⅕ ⅕ ⅕ ⅕
⅙ ⅙ ⅙ ⅙ ⅙ ⅙
⅐ ⅐ ⅐ ⅐ ⅐ ⅐ ⅐
⅛ ⅛ ⅛ ⅛ ⅛ ⅛ ⅛ ⅛
⅑ ⅑ ⅑ ⅑ ⅑ ⅑ ⅑ ⅑ ⅑
1/10 1/10 1/10 1/10 1/10 1/10 1/10 1/10 1/10 1/10

2. Loop the **greater** fraction. Use the fraction wall to help.

$\frac{1}{9}$ or $\frac{1}{7}$	$\frac{7}{10}$ or $\frac{7}{9}$	$\frac{3}{4}$ or $\frac{7}{8}$	$\frac{7}{8}$ or $\frac{5}{6}$	$\frac{2}{3}$ or $\frac{5}{7}$

3. Write each group of fractions in order (from smallest to largest).

$\frac{1}{5}$ $\frac{1}{9}$ $\frac{1}{8}$	$\frac{2}{7}$ $\frac{2}{5}$ $\frac{2}{9}$	$\frac{5}{6}$ $\frac{9}{10}$ $\frac{7}{8}$
....	....	....
$\frac{3}{4}$ $\frac{2}{3}$ $\frac{1}{2}$	$\frac{3}{8}$ $\frac{1}{3}$ $\frac{3}{10}$	$\frac{3}{5}$ $\frac{3}{4}$ $\frac{5}{9}$
....	....	....

Ordering fractions
(Follows *Giant Discussion Book* page 24.)

Name ....

For each event:
- write the three lengths for each team in order (from smallest to greatest).
- write all six lengths in order.

Shotput

Blue team
- Owen 7.23 m
- Shahid 7.32 m
- Tania 6.98 m

Red team
- Amber 6.90 m
- Glen 7.20 m
- Sonja 7.02 m

6.98 m

6.90 m

Javelin

Blue team
- Owen 22.15 m
- Shahid 21.90 m
- Tania 20.42 m

Red team
- Amber 23.15 m
- Glen 20.75 m
- Sonja 21.80 m

Discus

Blue team
- Owen 18.30 m
- Shahid 17.42 m
- Tania 18.15 m

Red team
- Amber 17.65 m
- Glen 17.95 m
- Sonja 17.80 m

Ordering decimals
(Follows *Giant Discussion Book* page 25.)

Name ....

To answer the riddle:
- figure out each angle and write it in the space
- write each letter above the matching angle (or angles) at the bottom of the sheet.

Riddle:
What do you get when you cross a chicken with a clock?

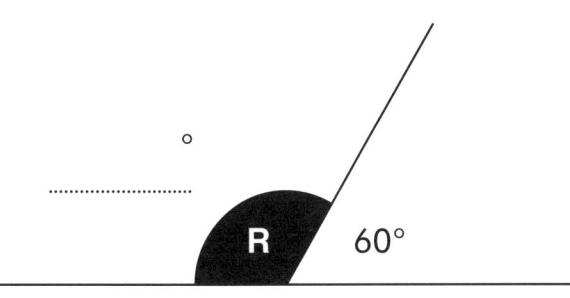

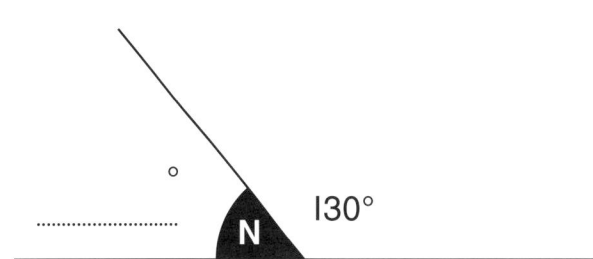

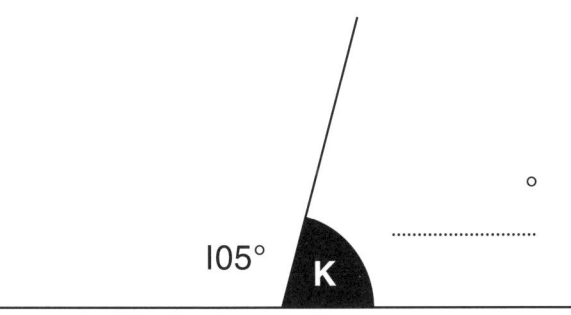

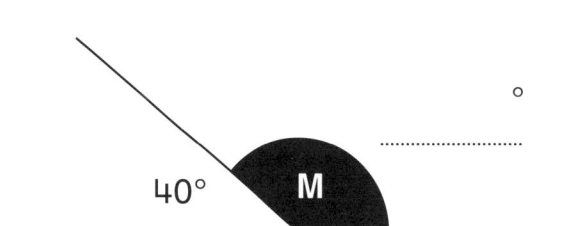

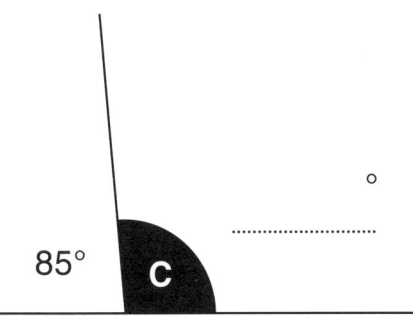

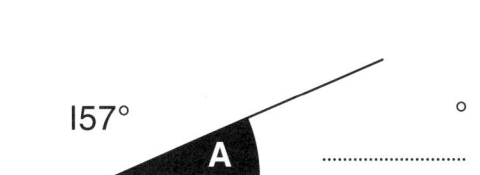

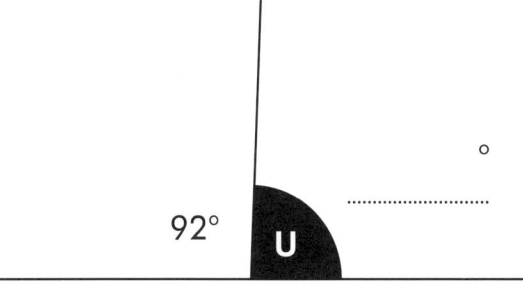

Answer:

....
23°   50°   23°   15°   23°   120°   140°   95°   15°   88°   95°   75°

Calculating angles in a straight line
(Follows *Giant Discussion Book* page 27.)   27

Name ....

Draw rotations of 90° (around each ●).

28 **Investigating patterns made by rotating shapes**
(Follows *Giant Discussion Book* page 28.)

Name ....

1. For each rectangle in the block below:
   - use a ruler to measure the length (l) and the width (w)
   - calculate the area (A)

blue	pink	purple
l = ... cm	l = ...	l = ... w = ...
w = ... cm	w = ...	A = ...
A = ... sq. cm	A = ...	green
red		
l = ... w = ...		l = ...
A = ...		w = ...
yellow	**brown**	**orange**	A = ...
l = ...	l = ...	l = ...	
w = ...	w = ...	w = ...	
A = ...	A = ...	A = ...	

2. Shade the rectangles in the colours shown.
   Then write the colours that match these clues.

Clue	Colour of ☐
Has the same area as the **pink** ☐.	
Has twice the area of the **pink** ☐.	
Has half the area of the **green** ☐.	
Has an area equal to the **purple** ☐ and **blue** ☐ together.	
Has an area equal to the **pink** ☐ and **red** ☐ together.	
Has one third the area of the **green** ☐.	

3. Calculate the area of the whole block of rectangles.

   l = ... w = ... A = ...

Using square centimetres 29
(Follows *Giant Discussion Book* page 29.)

Name ....

1. Complete the table for these bags of sweets.

	500 g	250 g	200 g	125 g	100 g	50 g
Number of bags filled from 1 kg	2					
Fraction of 1 kg in each bag	$\frac{1}{2}$					

2. How many 50 g could be filled from:

$\frac{1}{2}$ kg sweets?	$\frac{1}{4}$ kg sweets?	$\frac{1}{10}$ kg sweets?	$\frac{3}{4}$ kg sweets? ....

3. Figure out how many 100 g could be filled from these amounts.
   (Write any amounts of sweets left over.)

$\frac{1}{4}$ kg sweets	$1\frac{1}{2}$ kg sweets	$\frac{3}{4}$ kg sweets	1.2 kg sweets
.... 100 g bags	.... 100 g bags	.... 100 g bags	.... 100 g bags
.... g left	.... left	.... left	.... left

4. Draw four different bags of sweets you could fill from exactly:

1 kg of sweets	
0.6 kg of sweets	

Relating grams to the kilogram
(Follows *Giant Discussion Book* page 30.)

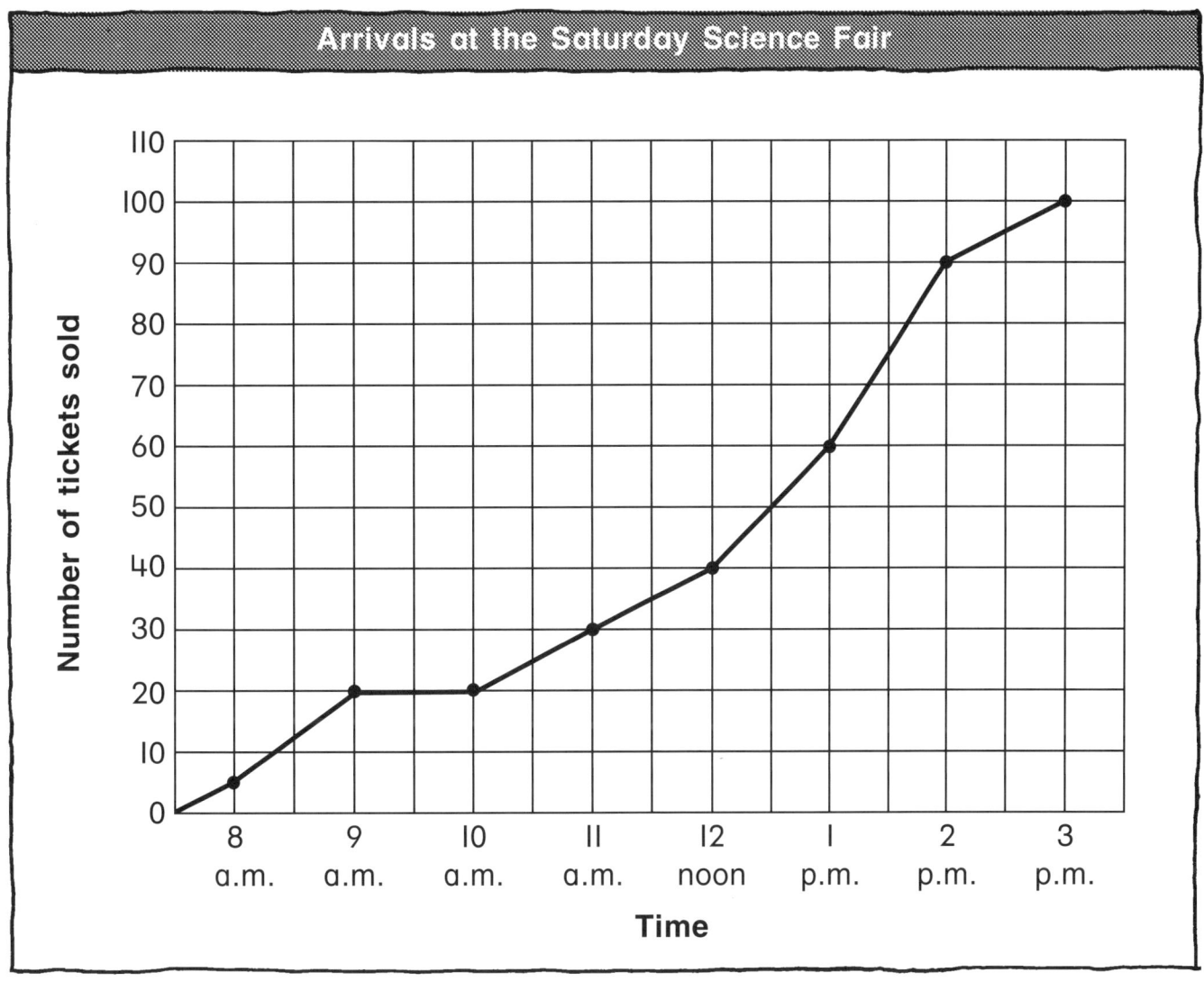

1. How many tickets had been sold by:

    • 8 a.m.? .... • noon? .... • 2 p.m.? ....

2. How many people altogether attended the fair? ....

3. How many tickets were sold between:

    • 10 a.m. and 11 a.m.? ....   • noon and 1 p.m.? ....

    • 8 a.m. and 9 a.m.? ....   • 9 a.m. and 10 a.m.? ....

4. Why is the line horizontal between 9 a.m. and 10 a.m.?

   ....

5. During which **hour** was the **greatest** number of tickets sold? .... to ....
   What do you notice about the line for that hour?

   ....

Interpreting data in a line graph

(Follows *Giant Discussion Book* page 31.)

Name ....

1. Calculate the cost of each of these purchases.

Biscuits and Snack Pack	Margarine and Sultana Flakes	Ice cream and Chocolate Sauce	Lemon Cordial and Orange Juice
Total	Total	Total	Total ....

2. Figure out the **difference** between the price of these items.

Sultana Flakes and Margarine	Ice cream and Orange Juice	Ice cream and Chocolate Sauce	Lemon Cordial and Biscuits
Difference	Difference	Difference	Difference ....

3. Calculate the total cost of the 3 most expensive items.

....

Extending written methods for decimals
(Follows *Giant Discussion Book* page 32.)

Name ....

1. Write each of these numbers in the correct 'bin'.

(15) (18) (20) (24) (30) (36)
 (38) (50) (75) (93) (100)
(120) (124) (128) (150) (160) (161)

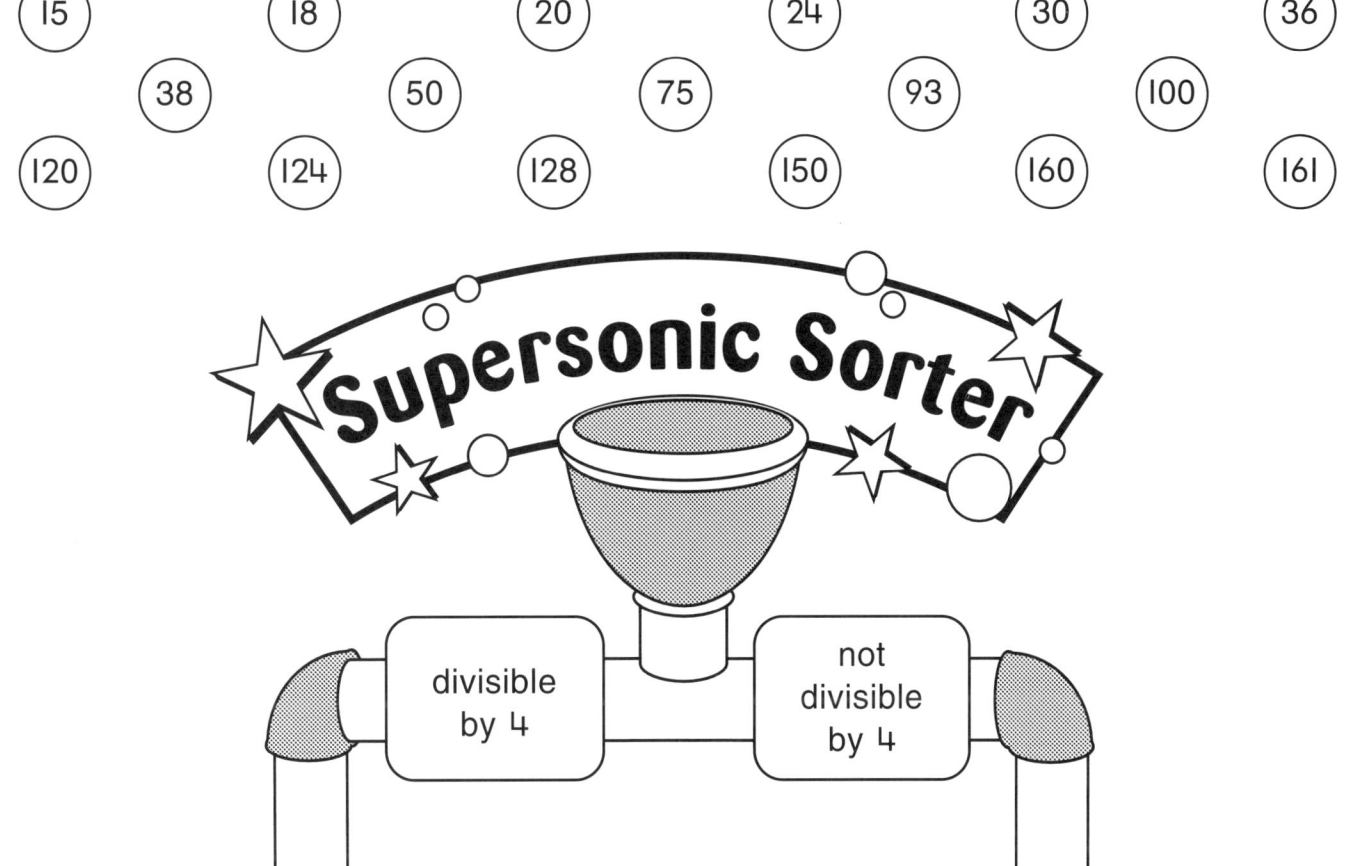

2. Which bins hold odd numbers? .... and ....

Which bins hold multiples of 10? .... and ....

3. Write an extra number in each bin.

4. Loop each number that is divisible by 3.

Applying tests for divisibility
(Follows *Giant Discussion Book* page 33.)

Name ....

1. Calculate the number of people who could board the giant Ferris wheel during these time periods.
   Show your working.

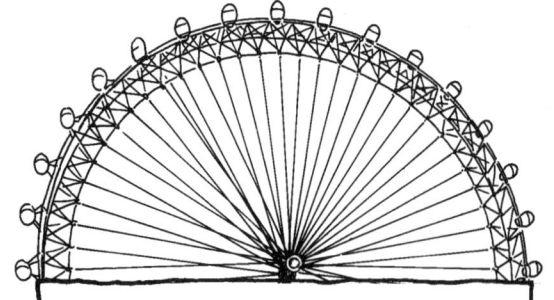

30 minutes	
1 hour	
one day in summer	

Prices
Adults   £8.50
Children £5.00

Opening hours
1 April to 10 September
8:30 a.m. to 10 p.m.

11 September to 31 March
9:30 a.m. to 6 p.m.

Data
32 carriages
25 people per carriage
30 minutes for one revolution of the wheel.

2. Use your answers from question 1 to help calculate the amount of money taken for each time period.

Time period	Suppose **all** people are adults	Suppose **half** the people are children and half are adults
30 minutes		
1 hour		
one day in summer		

Developing calculator skills
(Follows *Giant Discussion Book* page 34.)

Name ....

1. Complete the tables so that each answer is written in three different ways.
   (Use the patterns to help.)

Division	Answer		
437 ÷ 4	109 r 1	109 $\frac{1}{4}$	109.25
438 ÷ 4	109 r 2		
439 ÷ 4			
440 ÷ 4			
441 ÷ 4			
442 ÷ 4			

Division	Answer		
437 ÷ 5	87 r 2	87 $\frac{2}{5}$	87.4
438 ÷ 5			
439 ÷ 5			
440 ÷ 5			
441 ÷ 5			
442 ÷ 5			

2. Calculate the monthly payments.
   (Decide on the most suitable way to write the remainders.)

Make equal payments over 4 or 5 months

	4 payments	5 payments
£678 (computer)	4)678	5)678
£373 (television)	4)373	5)373

Expressing a quotient as a fraction or decimal

(Follows *Giant Discussion Book* page 35.)

Name ....

1. Complete these multiplication charts.

28 × 2	28 × 3	28 × 4
28 × 20	28 × 30	28 × 40

36 × 2	36 × 3	36 × 4
36 × 20	36 × 30	36 × 40

2. Use the charts to help solve these problems. Show your working.

A bus tour costs £28 per person. How much is that for a bus-load of 32 people?
 	
    28
  × 32
  ――
	A school excursion costs £36 per pupil. How much is that for a class of 42 children?	Entry to a fun park costs £28 altogether. How much will 24 pupils pay?

A bus has 36 seats. It makes 34 trips each week. How many people can it carry in one week?	A theatre has 28 rows of seats, with 44 seats in each row. How many seats are in the theatre?	At a busy airport, 36 planes land every hour. How many planes could land in 24 hours?

Using long multiplication
(Follows *Giant Discussion Book* page 36.)

Name ....

Special Discount
If you spend between:
- £76 and £100, take off £15
- £51 and £75, take off £10
- £40 and £50, take off £5

Vikings £26.50
Early People £19.50
Pyramids £39.00
Inventions £21.00
Knights £15.55
The Aztecs £23.50
Roman Britain £25.50

1. Calculate the cost of these purchases.
   (Dont forget the discount!)

Pyramids and **Knights**	**Inventions**, **Vikings** and **Roman Britain**	**The Aztecs**, **Roman Britain** and **Early People**

2. Solve these problems. (Remember the discount!)

You have £50. If you buy **Inventions** and **Early People**, how much more would you need to buy **Knights** as well?	What is the **greatest** number of books you can buy with £100? (List the books.)

Solving real-life problems: money
(Follows *Giant Discussion Book* page 37.)

Name ....

Write each length as a fraction of a metre (on the left of the tape measure) and as a decimal (on the right).

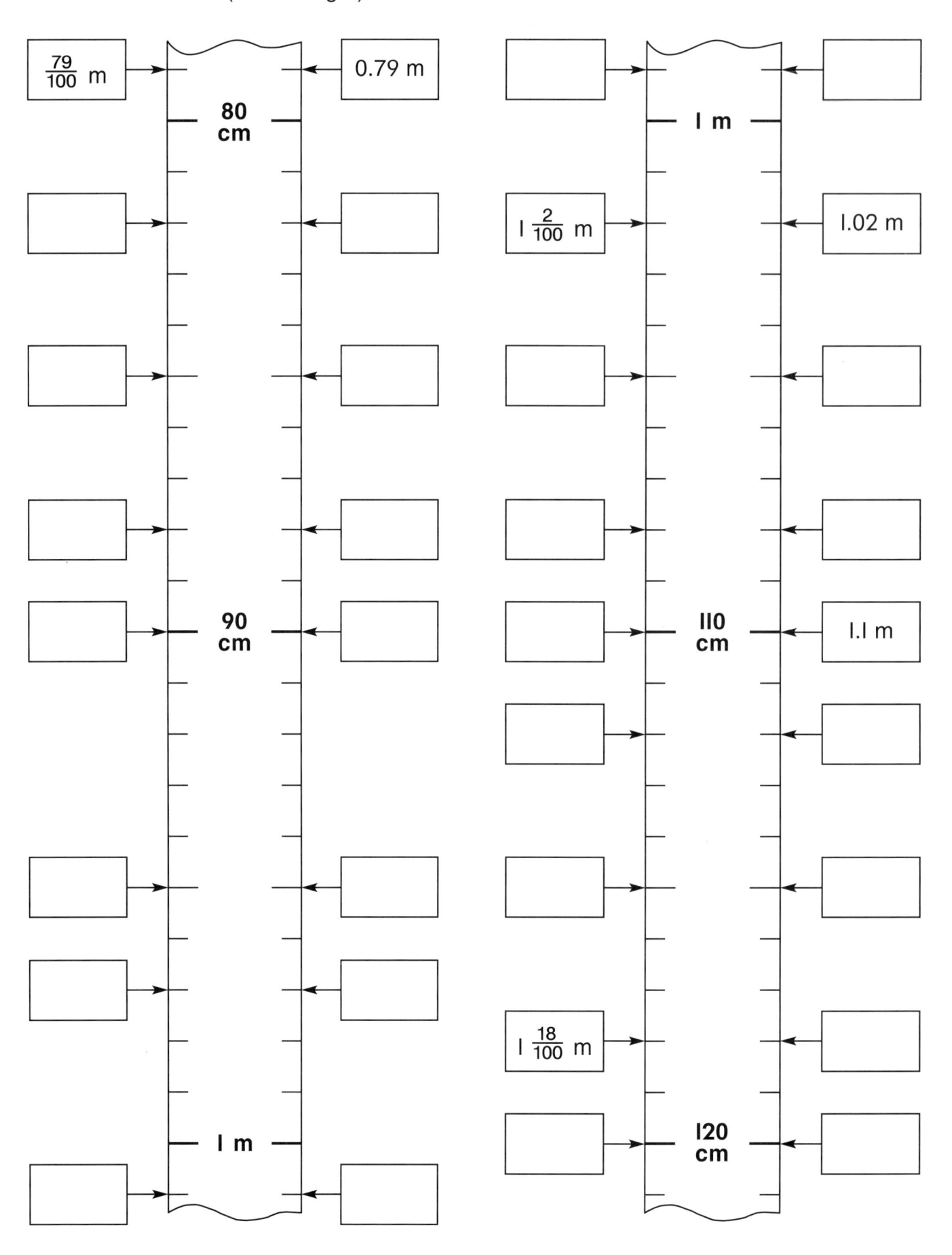

Tape measure 1 (left): marks at 80 cm, 90 cm, 1 m

- $\frac{79}{100}$ m → ← 0.79 m (at 79 cm)
- 80 cm
- 90 cm
- 1 m

Tape measure 2 (right): marks at 1 m, 110 cm, 120 cm

- 1 m
- $1\frac{2}{100}$ m → ← 1.02 m (at 102 cm)
- 110 cm — ← 1.1 m
- $1\frac{18}{100}$ m (at 118 cm)
- 120 cm

38 **Relating fractions and decimals**
(Follows *Giant Discussion Book* page 38.)

Name ....

1. Complete these mix-and-match puzzles.
   (Show each fraction as a picture, hundredths fraction, decimal and percentage.)

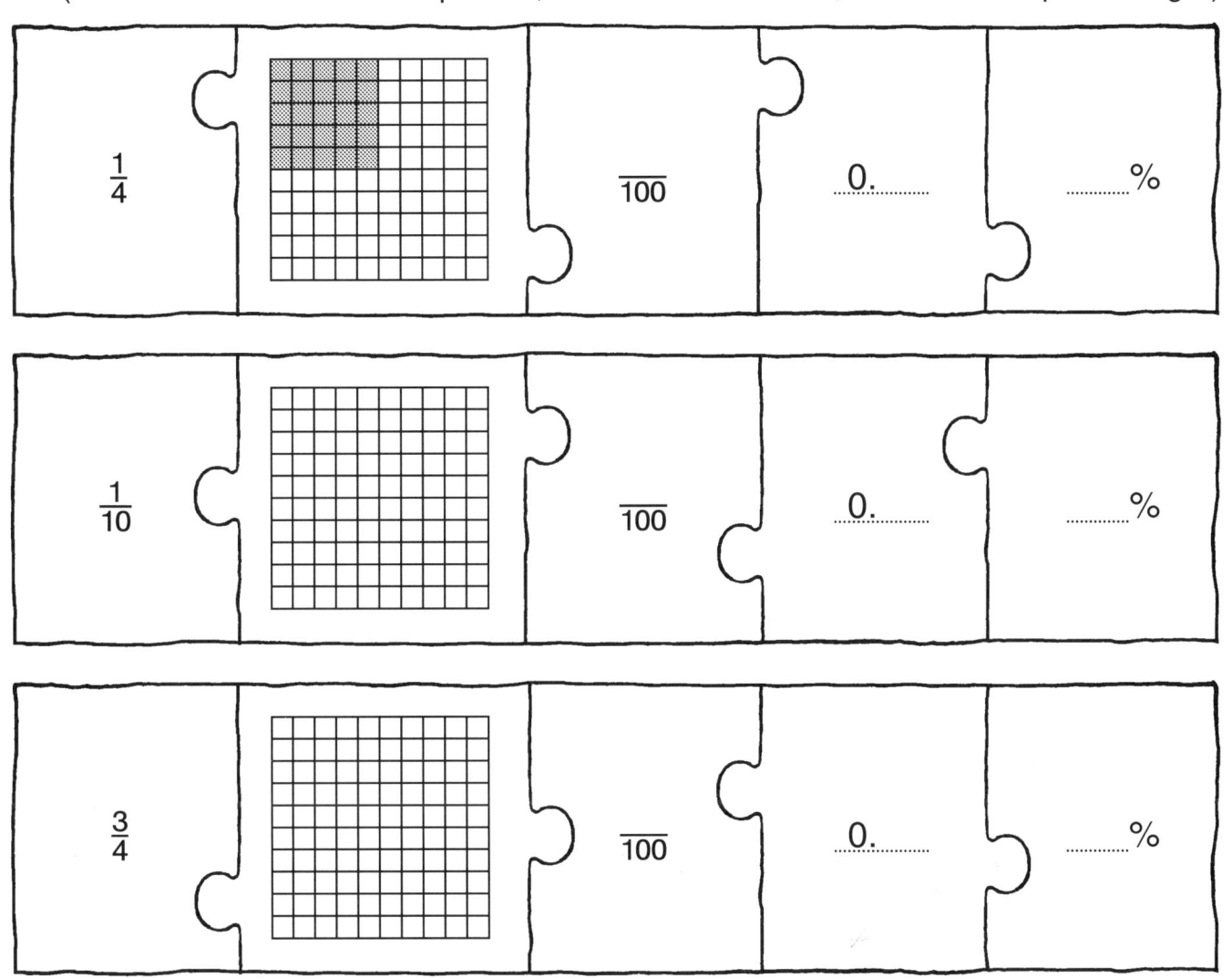

| $\frac{1}{4}$ | [grid picture] | $\frac{}{100}$ | 0.......... | ....% |

| $\frac{1}{10}$ | [grid picture] | $\frac{}{100}$ | 0.......... | ....% |

| $\frac{3}{4}$ | [grid picture] | $\frac{}{100}$ | 0.......... | ....% |

2. Figure out each of these amounts. Show your working.

| 25% of £40 | 10% of £50 |

| 50% of £80 | 25% of £200 |

Finding a simple percentage of a whole number

(Follows *Giant Discussion Book* page 39.)

Name ....

1. Write the missing numbers.

FOOTBALL CARDS
Buy 4 cards – get one free!

Buy 8 cards and get .... free.

Buy 20 cards and get .... free.

Buy 36 cards and get .... free.

Buy .... cards and get 3 free.

Buy .... cards and get 7 free.

Buy .... cards and get 10 free.

For 15 cards altogether, buy .... and get .... free.

For 30 cards altogether, buy .... and get .... free.

For 45 cards altogether, buy .... and get .... free.

2. Write the missing numbers.

FOOTBALL BADGES
Buy 5 badges – get one free!

Buy 10 badges and get .... free.

Buy 25 badges and get .... free.

Buy 45 badges and get .... free.

Buy .... badges and get 3 free.

Buy .... badges and get 7 free.

Buy .... badges and get 12 free.

For 12 badges altogether, buy .... and get .... free.

For 24 badges altogether, buy .... and get .... free.

For 42 badges altogether, buy .... and get .... free.

Working with ratio and proportion
(Follows *Giant Discussion Book* page 40.)

Name ....

1. Calculate the **range** for each set of data.
   (Write a number sentence to show your working.)

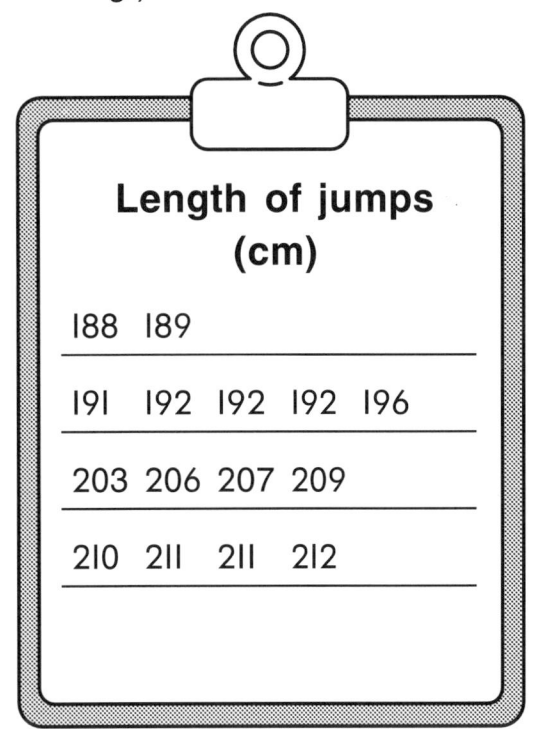

Number of skips without stopping

28	29				
32	35	36	36	36	38
41	44	44	47	49	
52	55				

Length of jumps (cm)

188	189			
191	192	192	192	196
203	206	207	209	
210	211	211	212	

Range: ....

Range: ....

2. Rewrite these times to make it easier to find the range.

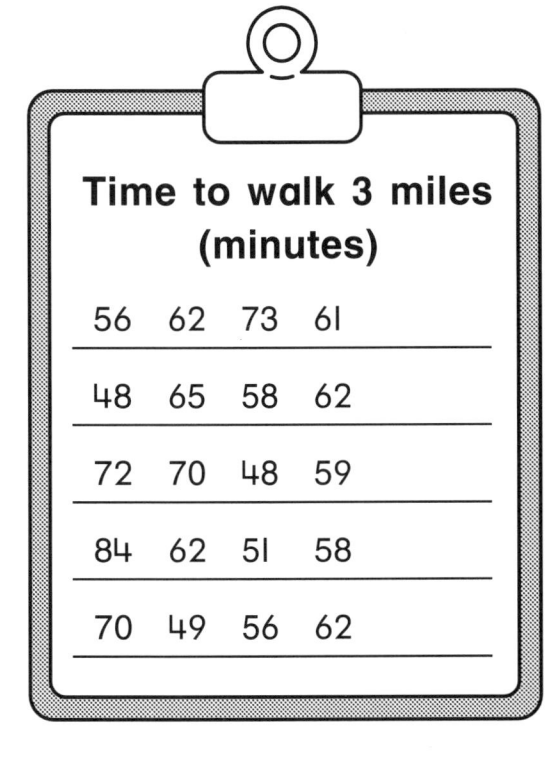

Time to walk 3 miles (minutes)

56	62	73	61
48	65	58	62
72	70	48	59
84	62	51	58
70	49	56	62

Time to walk 3 miles (minutes)

....

....

....

....

....

Range: ....

3. Loop the **mode** in each set of data.

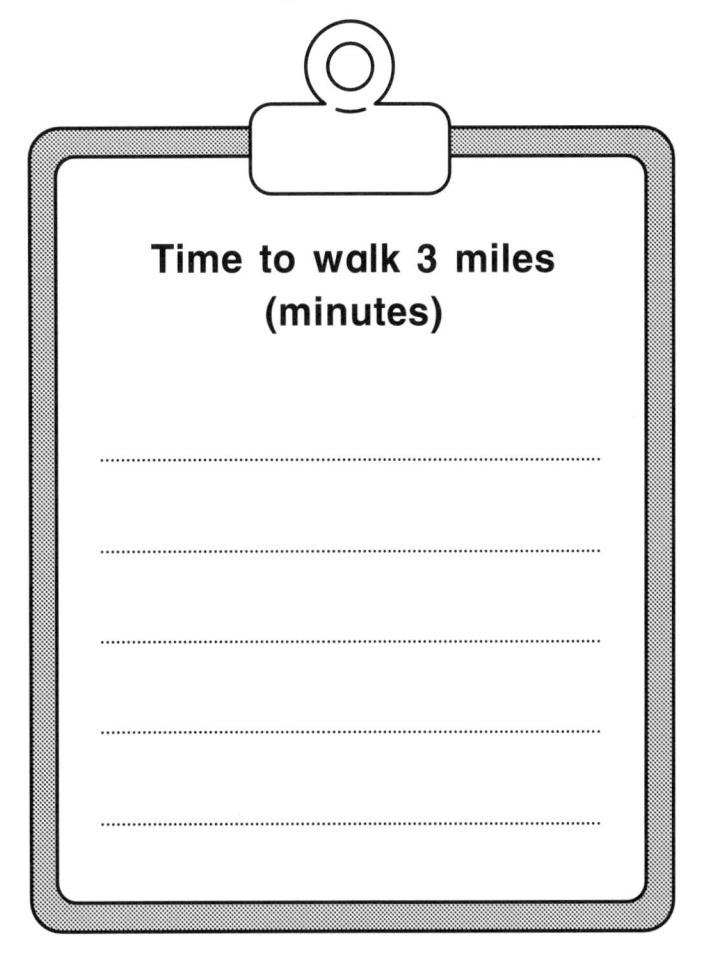

Finding the mode and the range
(Follows *Giant Discussion Book* page 41.)

Name ....

1. Draw the reflection of each shape in the nearby line.

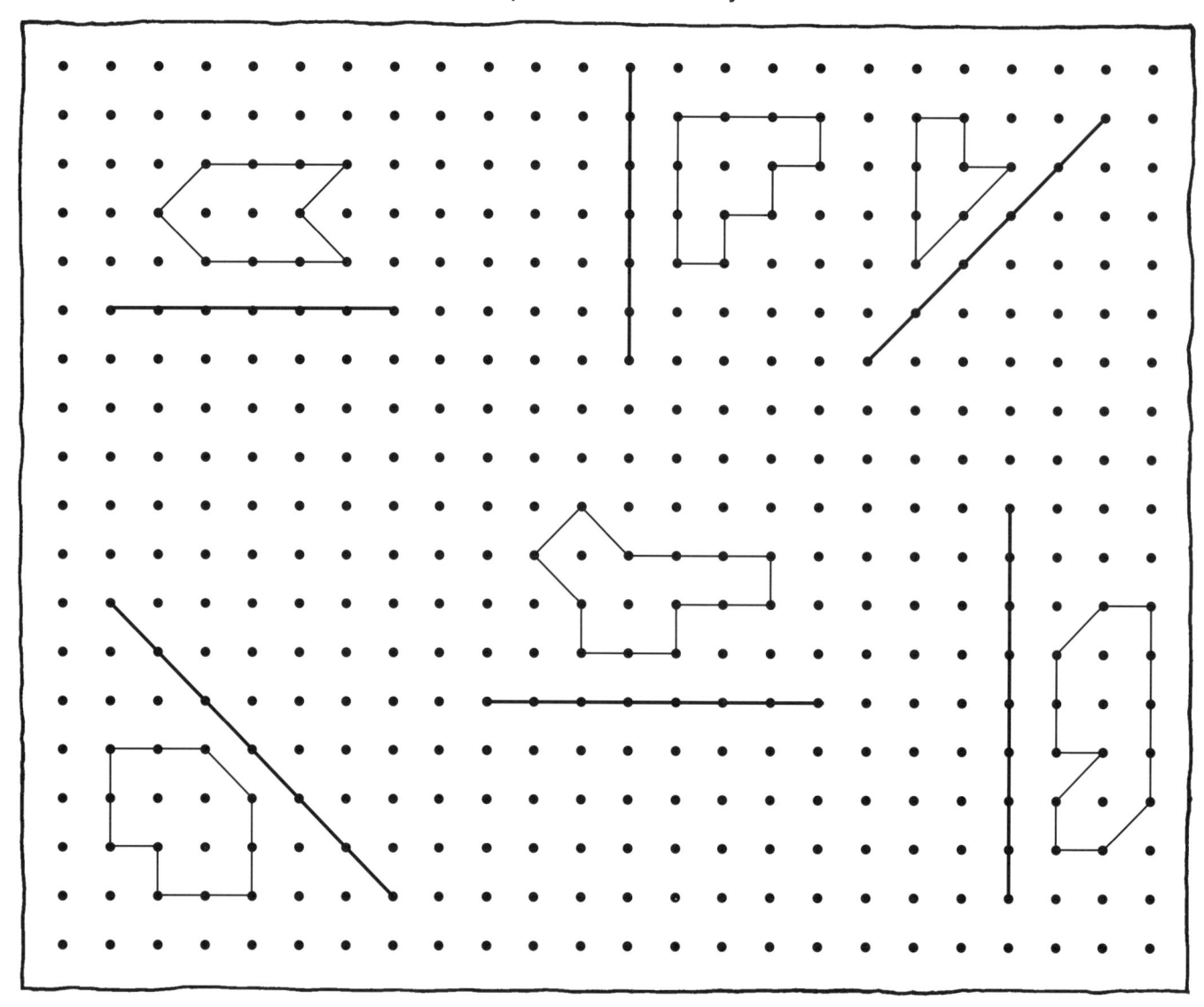

2. Draw these reflections in both lines of symmetry.

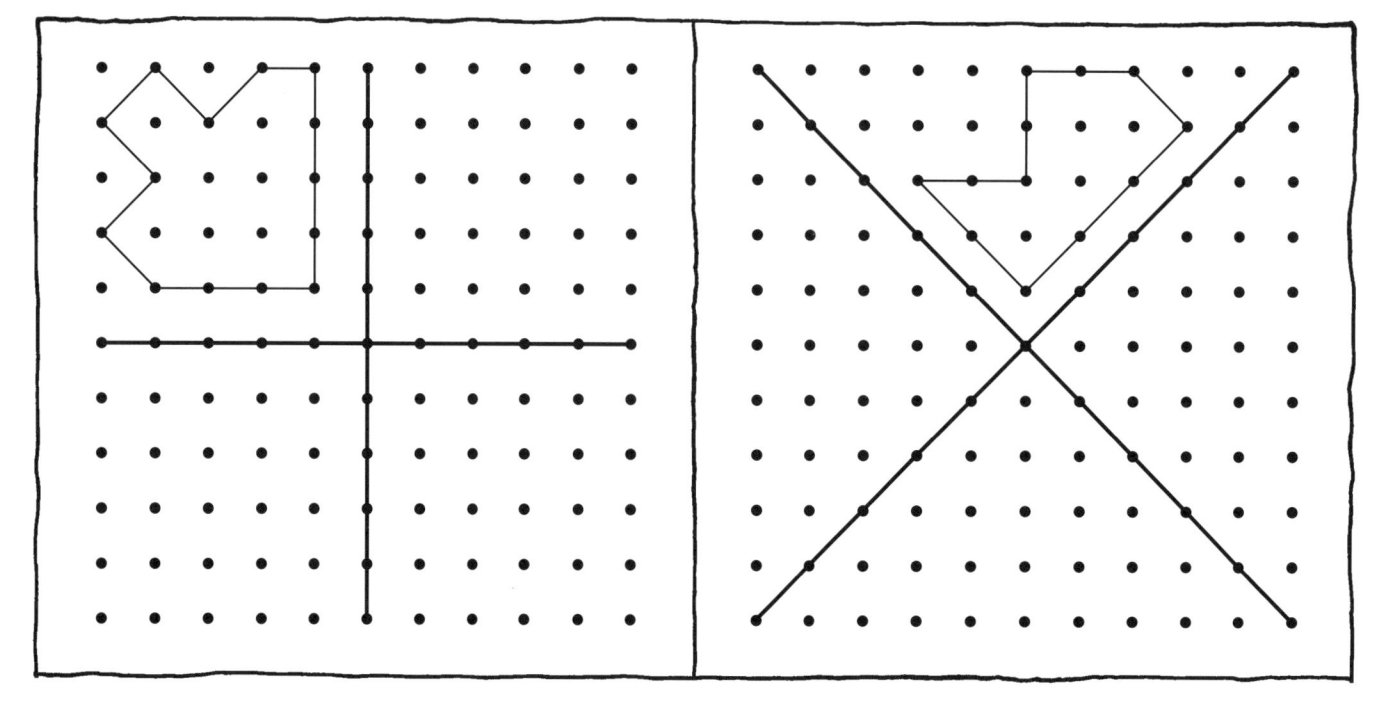

Reflecting shapes in one or two lines
(Follows *Giant Discussion Book* page 42.)

Name ....

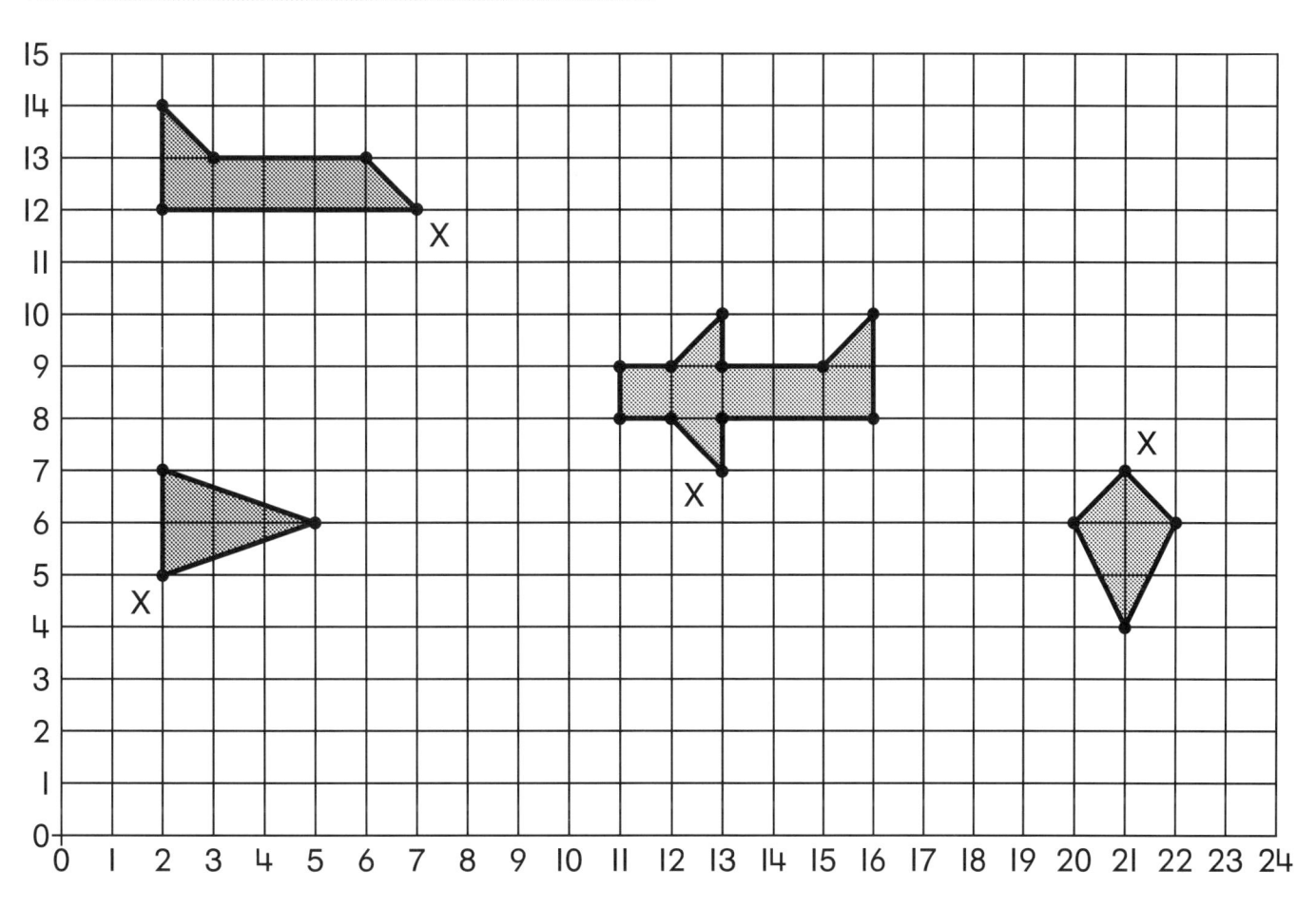

Draw each shape after the translation. (You could begin by moving the point X.)
Write the new co-ordinates of the points shown.

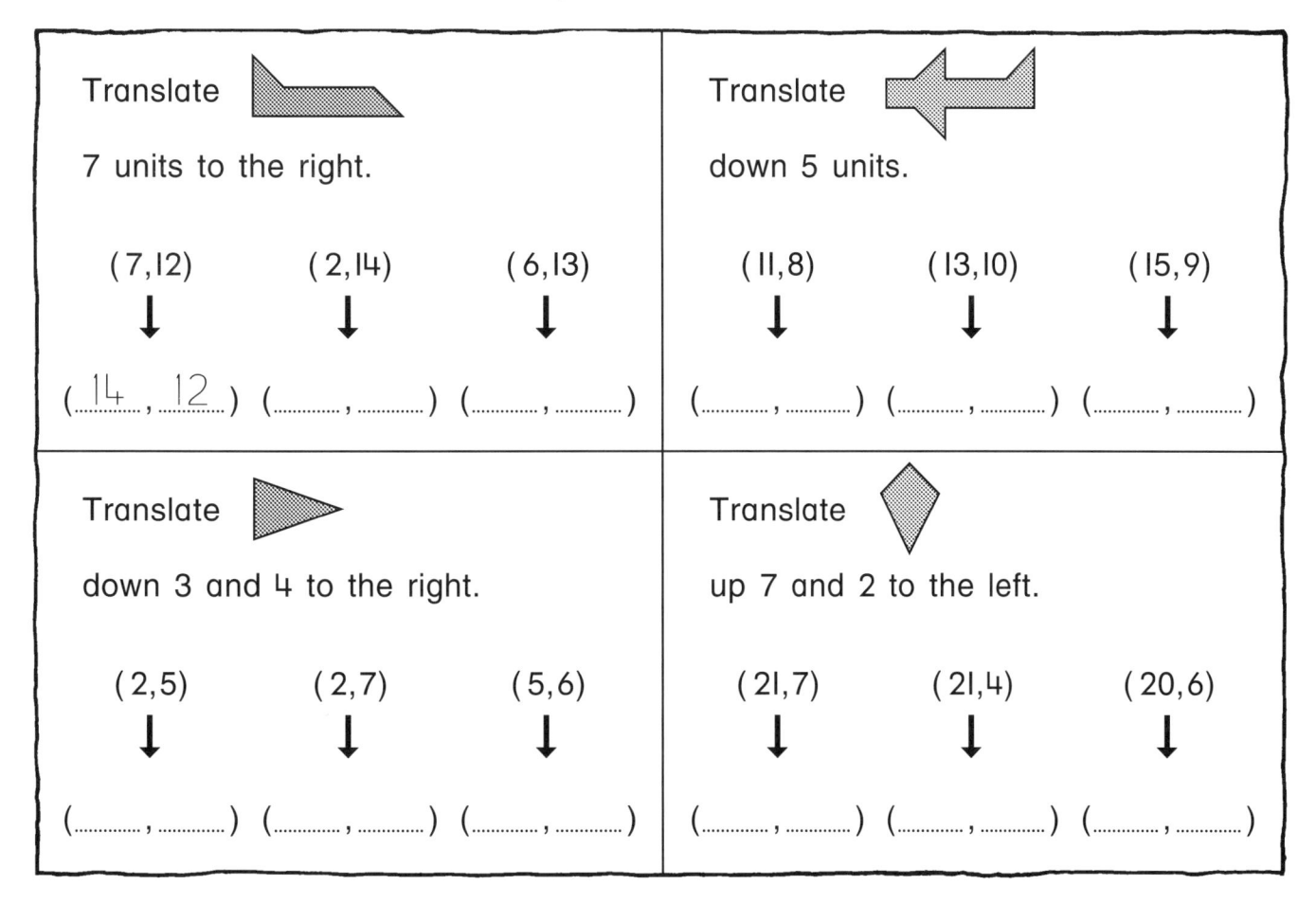

Translate [shape]

7 units to the right.

(7,12)   (2,14)   (6,13)
  ↓   ↓   ↓
(.14., .12.) (......,......) (......,......)

Translate [shape]

down 5 units.

(11,8)   (13,10)   (15,9)
  ↓   ↓   ↓
(......,......) (......,......) (......,......)

Translate [shape]

down 3 and 4 to the right.

(2,5)   (2,7)   (5,6)
  ↓   ↓   ↓
(......,......) (......,......) (......,......)

Translate [shape]

up 7 and 2 to the left.

(21,7)   (21,4)   (20,6)
  ↓   ↓   ↓
(......,......) (......,......) (......,......)

Making translations 43
(Follows *Giant Discussion Book* page 43.)

Name ....

Lancaster City Bus Timetable*							
Gardens	Leisure Centre	Hockley Rd	Goose Gate	Council House	Royal Centre	James St	Derby Rd
5:55 a.m.	6:05	6:10	6:25	6:35	6:50	7:05	7:35
6:15 a.m.	6:25	6:35	6:55	7:05	7:15	7:35	8:05
6:30 a.m.	6:40	6:50	7:10	7:25	7:35	7:55	8:25
6:45 a.m.	6:55	7:05	7:25	7:40	7:50	8:10	8:40
7:55 a.m.	8:10	8:20	8:45	9:00	9:10	9:30	10:00
8:55 a.m.	9:10	9:20	9:45	9:55	10:05	10:25	10:55
10:05 a.m.	10:20	10:30	10:50	11:00	11:10	11:30	12:00

* Times shown are not actual bus times.

LEISURE CENTRE

6:12

How long will Kym have to wait for the next bus?

....

By how many minutes did she miss the previous bus?

....

How long does the 6:45 bus from Gardens take to get to Derby Rd?

....

How much longer does the 7:55 take?

....

Is the travel time between Hockley Rd and Goose Gate always the same? ....

Write two different trips that each take one hour.

From ....   From ....

to ....   to ....

on the .... a.m. bus.   on the .... a.m. bus.

How long does the 6:40 bus from the Leisure Centre take to get to:

• Hockley Rd?   • Council House?

....

• James St?   • Derby Rd?

....

To get to Derby Rd by 9:00 a.m., what time would you catch the bus from:

• Gardens? ....

• Goose Gate? ....

Using a bus timetable

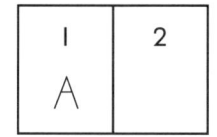

Name ....

To decode the riddle's answer, join each **fraction** of a litre to the matching amount in **millilitres**. (The number in the ▭ tells you where to write the letter from the ◁.)

Riddle

What do you call a cat with eight legs?

Fraction	#		Letter	ml
½ l	1		N	100 ml
1/10 l	2		O	1500 ml
¼ l	3		C	750 ml
¾ l	4		P	1250 ml
1/100 l	5		S	1010 ml
1½ l	6		A	500 ml
1¼ l	7		S	1750 ml
1 1/10 l	8		T	10 ml
1¾ l	9		U	1100 ml
1 1/100 l	10		O	250 ml

Answer

1	2
A	

3	4	5	6

—

7	8	9	10

Knowing the relationships between units of capacity 45
(Follows *Giant Discussion Book* page 45.)

Name ....

1. Calculate these distances.
   (Show your working.)

Oxford to Nottingham
Coventry to Leeds
Newcastle to Leicester

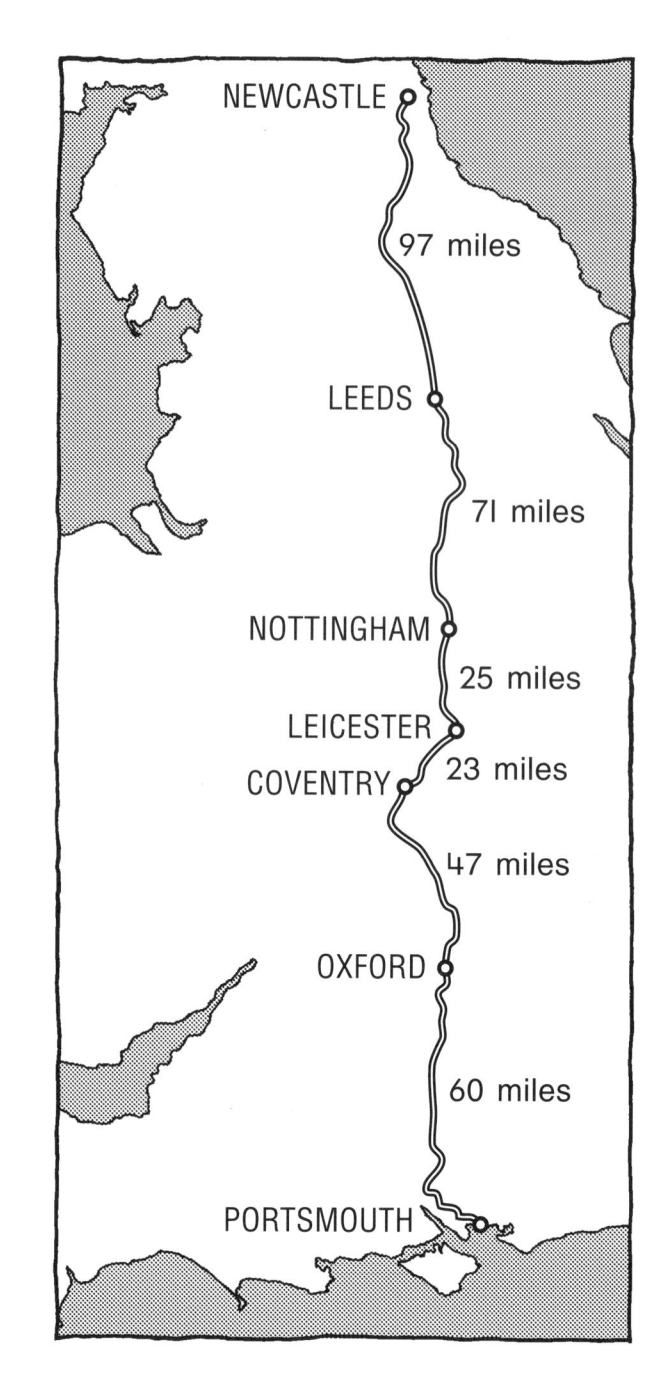

   Map:
   - NEWCASTLE
   - 97 miles
   - LEEDS
   - 71 miles
   - NOTTINGHAM
   - 25 miles
   - LEICESTER
   - 23 miles
   - COVENTRY
   - 47 miles
   - OXFORD
   - 60 miles
   - PORTSMOUTH

2. Solve these problems. (Show your working.)

Is Nottingham closer to Newcastle or Portsmouth? How much closer?	Is the distance from Portsmouth to Newcastle more or less than 300 miles? How many miles more or less?

   Adding three or more numbers
   (Follows *Giant Discussion Book* page 46.)

Name ....

1. Figure out these **discounts**.

	 £80 (skateboard)	 £120 (rollerblades)	 £200 (bike)
10% discount	£8		
20% discount			
25% discount			

2. Write the **discount** and then figure out the **sale price**.

£40 (football)
10% discount: ....
Sale price: ....

£100 (skateboard)
25% discount: ....
Sale price: ....

£60 (shoe)
25% discount: ....
Sale price: ....

£180 (bike)
50% discount: ....
Sale price: ....

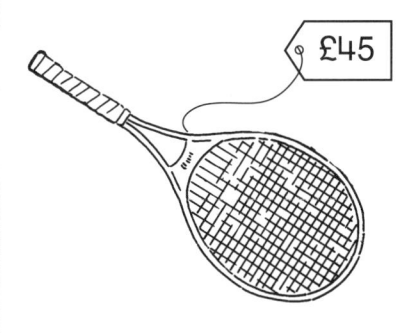

£45 (tennis racket)
10% discount: ....
Sale price: ....

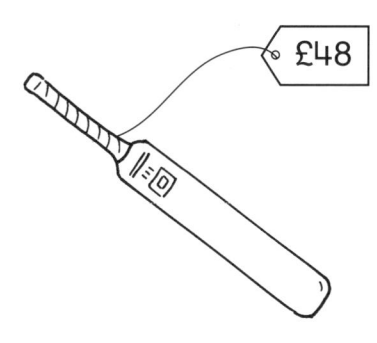

£48 (cricket bat)
25% discount: ....
Sale price: ....

Solving real-life problems: percentages
(Follows *Giant Discussion Book* page 47.)

Name ....

Use each factor 'tree' to help you find the pairs of factors.

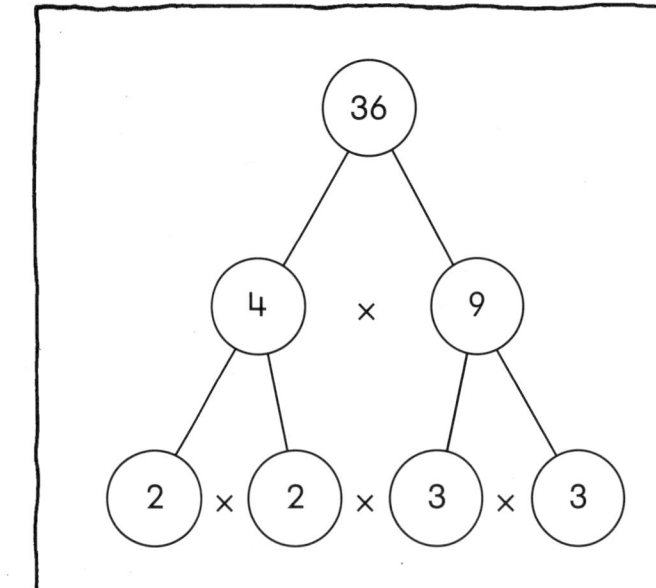

Factors of 36: __1__ × __36__

$2 \times (2 \times 3 \times 3)$ = __2__ × __18__

$(2 \times 2) \times (3 \times 3)$ = _____ × _____

$(2 \times 3) \times (2 \times 3)$ = _____ × _____

$3 \times (2 \times 2 \times 3)$ = _____ × _____

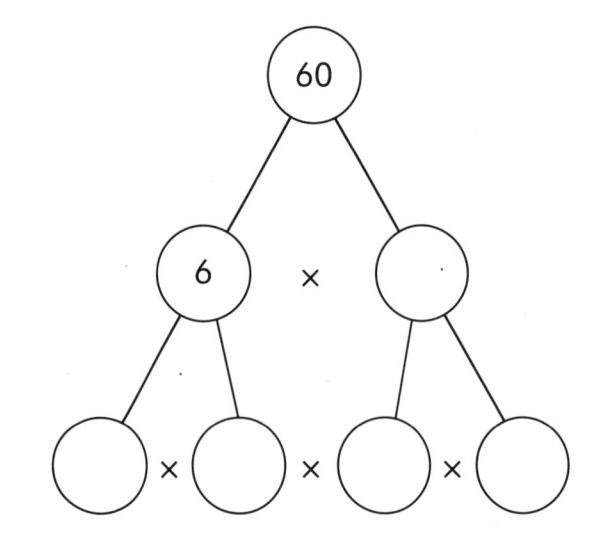

Factors of 60: _____ × _____

$2 \times (3 \times 2 \times 5)$ = _____ × _____

$3 \times (2 \times 2 \times 5)$ = _____ × _____

$5 \times (2 \times 2 \times 3)$ = _____ × _____

$(2 \times 3) \times (2 \times 5)$ = _____ × _____

$(2 \times 2) \times (3 \times 5)$ = _____ × _____

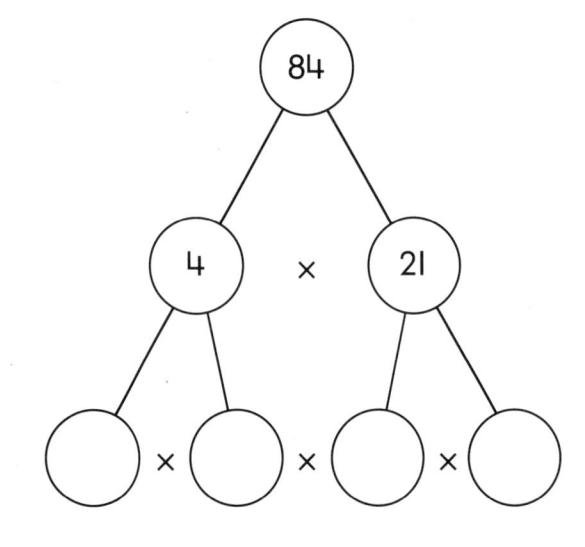

Factors of 84: _____ × _____

_____ = _____ × _____

_____ = _____ × _____

_____ = _____ × _____

_____ = _____ × _____

_____ = _____ × _____

Finding pairs of factors
(Follows *Giant Discussion Book* page 48.)